THEY MADE ME A PRIEST

JAMES DOHERTY

They made me a priest

THE COLUMBA PRESS
DUBLIN 1992

This edition, 1992, published by
THE COLUMBA PRESS
93 The Rise, Mount Merrion, Blackrock, Co. Dublin, Ireland

Cover by Bill Bolger
Origination by The Columba Press
Printed in Ireland by
Colour Books Ltd., Dublin

ISBN: 1 85607 048 4

ACKNOWLEDGEMENTS
A special word of thanks to Miss Mary Keogh, my housekeeper,
receptionist and carer, for her constant and faithful support and
encouragement. My thanks to Frs Brian Brady and Colm O'Doherty for
their critical reading of drafts and their continuing friendship.

*This book is dedicated to the Maynooth class of '67,
the men who helped make me a priest.*

All royalties from this book will go to
Foyle Hospice, Derry.

Contents

My own story   7
The Beginnings   14
The Training   24
The Spring   30
The Summer   47
Who supports the Priest?   56
Money   68
Authority   73
The Autumn   77
The Winter   93
The Future   102

My own story

It was a cold December day in 1966 and I was walking through the streets of Derry City, my birthplace and home town. I was a deacon then, just six months from ordination to the priesthood. Like all good deacons at that time, I was dressed in good clerical garb, black suit and stiff white collar. As I walked up this particular street, I saw coming towards me a young man who had been in primary school with me. I had lost touch with most young men of my age but I was still able to recognise them. I felt myself smiling as I looked forward to the greeting. When we were about ten yards from each other, my former school-mate bent his head away from me and lifted his hand to salute me as was the custom at that time in Derry for a man meeting a priest in the street. He did not look at me as a person but rather gave reverence to the collared figure. He was on his way past me when I called his name. He stuttered and grew embarrassed for a few moments until recognition dawned upon him. Then we talked and chatted and shared memories. He had married and was then the father of two children. He apologised for what could have been construed as impoliteness and then wished me well in my vocation.

That incident has always stayed with me and reminded me of a debate that had taken place back in Maynooth College about how clerical students and priests are cut off from the mainstream of life. One of the points made in the debate was the fact that one's very clothes cut one off from ordinary people.

This reminds me of a very simple event which happened several years earlier as my father and I were walking up O'Connell Street in Dublin. It was and still is a very busy street. It was not unusual to meet priests making the same walk. Every so often a man would salute or raise his cap as he passed the priests. My father quietly remarked, 'They must be from the north.' I was a little taken aback by the remark and asked what he meant. 'Only a northerner salutes a priest on the street,' was my father's simple but strange comment. I cannot testify to its truth or validity, but I know as a young man on the streets of Derry, one was expected to salute a priest on the street if such a meeting occurred. The reason given at that time was that the priest may be carrying the Blessed Sacrament and it was out of reverence to that that one saluted. I presume that in the cosmopolitan urbanised setting of Dublin city, a priest would just as easily be going to watch a film, attend the Abbey Theatre or be heading to Croke Park. I think my father's comment might have been saying more about him than about the religious practice or behaviour of the time.

It is said that the priest fills the role of communicator, that he is the one to preach the good news and that is more often than not translated as meaning preaching sermons on Sundays. Even there I doubt if we priests give the impression that we are preaching or talking about good news. Listening to people it seems that we are more concerned about moralising and teaching ethics than spreading a Gospel message that is consoling, uplifting and joyous. And to make it worse we carry out that exercise in a most boring way – boring in our use of language, in the tone of our voice, and in the content of the message which are trying to communicate.

This reminds me of a comment made to me by a very elderly gentleman. He said that priests can talk in beautiful terms about heaven and its joys and yet when we come to face death we are no more excited than the ordinary person.

In the last ten years I have become disabled because of Multiple Sclerosis and I know about uniting one's sufferings with Jesus, I know about surrendering oneself into the arms of God – these things I know in my head, but I know that my heart is not there yet. I would like to be able to offer up my sufferings to God with genuine sincerity and deep faith but I have to admit that my humanity seems to prevent me from doing this. I have stopped screaming at God but I still know of the small tear that sometimes trickles down my face. I believe that my God still loves me, is still with me, and his ever-prevading presence consoles me. I am sorry that I do not seem to be able to give him all my heart, all my soul, all my mind.

I wish I could – but then again I wish I were a saint, but I'm not. I feel at times that it can be hard for people to see priests as ordinary men. Do solicitors, bank-managers, teachers, and other 'white-collar' workers suffer the same difficulties? Or has it something to do with the fact that priests work in the 'God-field' and the sense of mystery which surrounds such work also surrounds the man who is a priest?

Are priests considered so divorced from life that people see us almost as 'aliens'? Is it the fact that we are celibate men which causes some misgivings? Then why should not all men who happen for whatever reason to be celibate feel distanced from real life? What is involved in a vocation to the priesthood? What is it that touches a man's inner heart to want to become a priest? Does a man get a special and particular audible calling from God himself? Or does he find his way into priesthood much in the same way as a person finds him/herself going into marriage – being influenced by his family, his friends and the community in general?

And yet many people would want the priest to be the 'holy' person who somehow can provide a link between them and the unknown and mysterious God. In this sort of context the priest may be caught by the unconscious and unexpressed perceptions and expectations of the people. One of these perceptions which I believe is quite widespread is that being 'holy' is in some strange way being better than the ordinary sinful human person. 'Holiness' is understood as having overcome one's human weaknesses. This can lead to a very mistaken idea that the man who becomes a priest does so because he is worthy of it, he has broken through the fallibility of his humanity. Some people still see the priest in this light; others see it as being so foolish that they have rejected the priest and all that he stands for as irrelevant; and then again many others do not even see it as a question. Some priests even live with silly ideas about their importance and specialness.

When I was an infant at school I can remember being accused of day-dreaming in class. While it is not the best way to learn, there is something precious about being able to dream (whether it happens by day or night). I would like to take a dreamy look at priesthood – dreamy only in the sense that I do not intend to offer this book as a closed, tightly fabricated document. I will be flitting in and out of issues that have crossed my path in priesthood and I would think that many a priest and lay person has also considered them from time to time. I hope to add to the debates which are on-going about the priest and his ministry. Thought and debate help to push out and broaden boundaries, especially those boundaries which have been allowed to fossilise.

People sometimes ask, 'What made you become a priest, Father?' I presume that such questioners may have the idea that there was some dazzling light or some hushed voice in the midst of prayer that initiated the call, whereas in fact it is usually people them-selves who began the journey. People like my father and mother for whom the practice of their faith was more important than their theological understanding of the mysteries of their faith; people like simple, gentle, dedicated priests whom I had met in my up-bringing; people like my neighbours who lived as a community without ever verbalising their relationship, who shared a cup of sugar or a bottle of milk when their larder ran out. And there were individuals who impressed me with very simple ways of behav-ing – like the old man who had not enough money to buy a decent coat, yet walked to Mass each Sunday and with one knee on his cap, blessed himself with a reverence that would shame many a cloistered nun. A question better than 'what made me a priest?' would be 'who made me a priest?' I remember the good faithful people among whom I lived … ordinary, hard-working people who struggled to pay their weekly bills and yet could be seen heading to Mass each Sunday morning. They were simple folk who respected each other. I believe that same quality of living can be found today among the Derry people, even in spite of the hell they have been living through for over twenty years. They have stirred something in my heart to serve them as their priest. God was a faithful God, a God who was content to be born in a stable in Bethlehem, a God who was at ease riding on a donkey, a God who did not look down on them because of their deprivation and diffi-culties. It was this God whom I wanted to get to know and to serve. I could not have spoken those words at the tender age of eighteen, yet the vision behind them was stirring in my heart even then.

The very first time the idea of being a priest came into my mind happened on my Confirmation Day. It did not happen in the Cathedral to which I was marched, along with about 800 other young children, to be confirmed by the bishop. Previous to the march I was standing in the play-ground of St Columba's Boys' School along with the other pupils to be confirmed. The teacher was putting us into lines and generally getting us ready for the big march. Just before we began, he suggested we sing a hymn. I still remember its title and a few of its words, 'A Message to the Sacred Heart.' The words which were etched on my heart that day were, 'My child, my child, give me thy heart, thy heart is all I need.' As I sang it out with great gusto I remember saying to myself, 'OK, God, I'll give you my heart – I'll be your priest.' Every so often over the next number of years, that memory kept coming back. I had then thought of other possibilities – to be a footballer like my father, to be a bricklayer like my brother-in-law – but coming to the end of my time in St Columb's College, the memory of my confirmation day seemed to have persisted. I made the decision to go to Maynooth College – not to be a priest, as that still seemed too ridiculous, but to give it a try, and if it failed I could always get some job. But the line had been cast and despite my struggling over the years, I was finally hooked, caught, and landed ... not by a dazzling light or a hushed voice in prayer but by a very simple desire to love a God who loved all people and to try in some uncertain way to serve God's people. It took the seven years in seminary for that desire to become strong enough to give me the courage to make the final decision on ordination day. During those seven years I was strongly influenced by the other young men who were studying and praying with me, by my family and friends with whom I would spend my few months holidays each year, and by my own prayer-life. I was prepared to accept the mantle of priesthood as I knew it then, but I was not prepared for the daily living out of that priesthood in parish. It took several years before I was able to ask myself some real and important questions. Even yet I can admit to not having all the answers; but I believe I have learned to ask myself some to the right questions – and living with the questions can be more important than struggling with a 'QED' answer.

Generally speaking I have good memories of priests whom I knew as a boy. Some of these taught me as a pupil at St Columb's College. In the main they were dedicated and good teachers. I'm sure every man has some bad memories of his teachers. I can honestly say that I was never struck or beaten by a priest at college even though I witnessed some very cruel beatings being given to other pupils. I got my fair share of punishments from the lay teachers, but I probably deserved them ... and memories are usually very prejudicial.

I can remember the priests of my parish as being very hard-working and silent men. Some of them had their bad tempers which they would take out on the altar-boys; but the bad-tempered ones were balanced by the gentler and quieter priests. On occasions I can remember them breaking into smiles and sharing some jokes with their people. They were good priests without any doubt, but they rarely showed their human faces. For some reason they always appeared closeted behind their clerical collars. As I grew into priesthood which I shared with them, I found them to be very human men whom I wanted to get to know. I am not excusing the bad-temperdness which I experienced from some of them when I was a boy; but I now know them to be human and fallible men just like myself. I am grateful for the memories of dedication, uprightness, and true perseverance. It can have been no easier for them to face the changes in the Church at the time of Vatican II than it was for the laity, and I believe they are to be admired for their willingness to undertake change. I often wonder how lonely it must have been for them at that time and wonder what helps were given to them in order to adjust to the changing face of the Church. They themselves had been reared in a very particular and straight-jacketed Church and they probably knew of no other way of being a priest. They carried out their functions and duties with great dedication and selflessness and I must admit that this helped me to the priesthood. Their role as sacrament-providers was very clear and they did that job extremely well ... but at what cost to themselves and their own humanity? This might be a very unreal question. They provided a service most efficiently, a service that was expected of them at that time in the Church. But both the Church and society have changed considerably over the past twenty years and the priest of today has to try to respond to the needs of society and the Church as best he can. I only pray that the priests of today are able to respond as well as the priests of former times.

The Beginnings

It was in 1960 that I had made the decision to enter a seminary to begin studies for the priesthood. In many ways the whole thing seemed like a dream. It would be easy now to say that I did not have a tremendous self-image, that I lacked confidence and did not really see myself as completing the course. I was particularly concerned about a very practical problem – could my family afford to keep me at College? In spite of the fact that I had a scholarship, there was quite a lot of things to be bought initially. I still remember with some humour receiving a list of clothes to be bought – black suit, black raincoat, black soutane, black shoes, black socks, black umbrella, black hat ... I wondered would the list include black underwear! Seven other students from Derry City, counties Tyrone, Fermanagh, Donegal, and Derry, were to join with me on that strange journey to Dublin. It was a financial struggle for my family to support me in my decision. In the few days before leaving on the train I received visits from uncles, aunts, and friends. Upon leaving my home they were pushing pound notes into my hands or pockets and wishing me well for the future. It was embarrassing to take such money and while my good friends would have been hurt if I had refused, there was also the thought within myself that such monies would make it easier for my family who could not have afforded to offer me pocket-money.

I had often wondered at that time how possible it would be for a young man from a working-class family to survive the financial demands. I think that if my mother had had received further education, she probably would have become an economist. How she managed to raise nine children on very low income was an amazing feat. Her budgeting began on a Friday night when the workers returned from their jobs with their earnings. The wage-packets were opened and the money spread out on the table. The appropriate money for such necessities as gas, electricity, rent, coal, milk was set aside. If any bills from the previous week were still outstanding, then they too were covered. Each working person in the family received his or her pocket-money ... and that included my father. A certain sum of money was also set aside for the 'chapel'. The remainder was then counted and this was budgeted for food for the next week. I would get a few pennies for cleaning my big brothers' shoes.

I grew up in this atmosphere and learned to appreciate the value of a penny. It was tough and hard and must have been a constant worry for my parents who shouldered their responsibilities with great perseverance and courage. It was the lot of many a working-class family at that time in Derry and 'keeping up with the Joneses' meant survival.

It must have been a funny-looking sight to see a group of young men, all dressed in sombre black, gather at the train station. The goodbyes were perfunctory and I think the embarrassment was felt more by the students than by the parents. So there was a sense of relief as the train pulled slowly out of Derry. There were four of us on the train and we were to gather the rest of our party as we journeyed south. It was then we were able to sit back and laugh at our appearance ... four young men with very little hard bristle on our chins and dressed up to look much older. There was no con-versation about why we were there or what brought us there. Instead we pulled out a pack of cards and, using match-sticks as money, we became involved in a few games of friendly poker. The journey to Dublin was long and as we approached the terminal station in Ireland's capital, the change in the atmosphere within the carriage became apparent. Thoughts were not expressed but I could hear myself asking 'What am I doing here?' We knew that we had to gather at Aston's Quay for the bus to Maynooth. We sauntered up O'Connell Street trying to look as inconspicuous as possible. We met a priest from the Derry diocese and he gave us a warm greeting. He turned to me and asked jocosely why I was not wearing my hat ... he probably saw it rolled up and held in a bun-dle under my arm.

It was easy to recognise the bus-station at Aston's Quay. A group

of young men dressed in clean black suits had already gathered. I
could not help wondering what had brought them all here. It
seemed a strange assembly. Greetings were short and stilted. The
bus journey along the narrow road to Maynooth College seemed
longer than the thirty minutes that it took to cover the distance.
The College campus was larger than anything that I had experienced. But I had arrived for better or for worse to begin discerning
the nature of 'my vocation'.

We followed the instructions of the Dean as he showed us to our
rooms and outlined a brief time-table for us. The rooms were built
in blocks of flats with strange-sounding names like Humanity,
Rhetoric, Logic and, having found Humanity Block, I soon discovered my room. While the room was small, holding a bed, a
wardrobe, a table and a chair, and a small sink unit, it looked quite
spacious to me. I never had a room to myself ... never mind a bed.
I had shared an attic with two double beds with my four brothers
since I was a boy and now, for the first time in my life, I had my
own space. There was the disadvantage that it was noiseless and
silent which created that sense of homesickness which everyone
must feel upon leaving home for the first time.

The bell, which was to sound out the day's time, called us to the
Chapel for prayer and notices. It was quickly pointed out to us
that the bell was to be known as *Vox Dei* (The Voice of God) and
our response was to be immediate and obedient.

One of the strangest and earliest memories I have was the wide
and varied selection of accents. I found my attempts to try to communicate with young men from Cork, Waterford, Tipperary were
almost as futile as trying to communicate with young men from
France, Italy or Germany. It took us more than a few days to begin
to learn to hear and listen to one another. But all of this was done
with a great sense of humour and fun and easy relationships were
quickly established.

Vox Dei soon began to dictate the time-table of the day. It was not
the most pleasant voice to hear at six o' clock in the morning but
one learns to adapt very quickly. In the early days and weeks we

would have been unaware of the sanctions we could have suffered by not responding to *Vox Dei* but they were soon pointed out to us. But we were busy those days finding out the geography of the place, getting to know exactly where various important areas were located – the chapel, the refectory, the notice-board, and the regular meeting places of the diocesan students. It soon became clear that while *Vox Dei* was an important voice, there was another voice that seemed to carry even more weight ... that of the Dean.

We were quickly taught that 'The Rule' was to be our guide in everything. And 'The Rule' was made up of many little rules, some of which we learned from reading the notice-board, more of which we learned from experience. There is no gainsaying the fact that it was tough ... but in some way I had expected it to be tough, probably an expectation born out of the idea that a priest's life was tough.

Many students found the rule of Solemn Silence rather difficult. It was a rule imposed with great severity and the breaking of it would make one liable to a severe reprimand ... total disregard for it would bring expulsion. In practical terms it meant that one was not allowed to speak from the beginning of the second night study period (about 8.15 p.m.) until after breakfast next morning. I did not mind the silent time in the morning as it took me some time to become fully awake, but some nights were very long.

Some of the rules must have seemed strange even to the authorities and while they were generally observed, I must admit to a tongue-in-cheek attitude among the general student body. We, as students, applied our own list of priorities to the rules. Smoking was forbidden within the College walls and I this was generally respected, although one might find the odd billow of smoke filtering from under the toilet doors. One was not allowed to enter another student's room but it was not unknown to see a few chairs gathered at the door of a student as we listened to music or just chatted together if the weather prevented us from enjoying the fresh air. There was one particular rule which I could never really understand which was enforced during my years of training (1960-1967) whereby a student was forbidden to remove a book from the library ... and the penalty was excomunication! We were also forbidden to have novels in our rooms and, as I was studying English for my degree course, I felt it to be important to read as widely as possible. So rather than risk excommunication I decided to smuggle books into the College ... I trust there is no such thing as retroactive punishment ... or maybe I'm simply trusting in the fact that the President of Maynooth today is also a classmate of mine.

Smuggling the books was not too much of a problem, but hiding them was a bit more difficult. I had a massive heavyweight wardrobe in my room which I was able to lift a few inches from the floor and, by having my book on the floor beside it, I was able to slip it underneath with a gentle push of the foot. I would have had a little piece of cord attached to the book so that I was able to extract the book fairly easily by tilting the wardrobe a little, placing my shoe on the cord and gently slipping the book away. I suppose all this seems rather complicated to the outsider, even in fact to the present day student, but our rooms were searched constantly and without warning and so we tried to take the necessary precautions. I wonder is that the reason why so many priests ordained before the seventies seem to be a little crafty!

Apart from the main rules of the institution, conformity and uniformity were regarded as essential to the running of the College. I still remember the long black line of students shuffling from the refectory to the Chapel reciting the *Miserere* psalm and the only distinguishing marks being hairstyle, spectacles and height (or lack of them). Singularity was definitely a grave misdemeanour. I suppose it could be argued that these rules did not help towards the personal development of the individual. And yet, contrawise, if a man were able to survive in spite of the rules, and use his own common-sense in the application of them, then it could be argued that he could learn a lot about self-discipline and discernment. I know several students who suffered a lot because of the rules and carried that suffering over into the priesthood and it took them a number of years to fully recover from their hurts.

I think it is sad that some priests have only unhappy memories of their student life. My most unhappy memory is when I was caught breaking some of the rules. I suppose the pertinent word in that previous sentence is the word 'caught'. My illicit novels were never found, my contraband (lemonade, chocolate, newspapers) were never discovered and my whispered messages during Solemn Silence were never heard. But I was caught.

There were many 'societies' that a student could join which were very useful during the dark winter evenings. I learned how to make leather wallets, leather covers for books; I learned the delicate techniques involved in picture-framing; but my main hobby was printing. In fact it became more than a hobby as the printing-society offered many services to the student-body.We printed programmes for concerts and plays, ordination cards for young ordinands and even Christmas cards for staff and students. We did not have access to word-processors in those days... every letter had to be set up by hand. It was a slow, meticulous job that demanded a lot of patience and not a little skill. Anyway I had been asked by the Dean to print out Night Prayer from the Breviary for use in the Chapel. This was a long, slow and tedious job and there were weeks when I had to allot my full free time to it. I was working at it one afternoon and I heard the warning bell for study. I knew I still had five minutes before the final bell and I thought I would be able to set up one more line before going to my room which was only two flights of stairs up from where I was working. I finished the line, smothered my hands in washing liquid, gave them a quick dry and then ran to get to my room. Just as I came to my corridor I heard the final bell clanging and then I skidded to a halt as there in front of me stood the Dean. He gave me an x-ray look, glanced at his watch but said nothing. When I reached my room I gave my hands a good wash, sat down at my desk and wondered would I receive a visit!

At about the same time in the College there was an epidemic of jaundice. The infirmary was quickly filled and so some of the students' rooms were requisitioned for service to the sick. I was in my room on this particular night and I was working. I discovered I needed a dictionary which the student across from my room possessed ... but Solemn Silence had started. So I had to face a moral dilemma. If I ventured over for the book, I would be breaking three rules: the Silence, entering another student's room and involving him in a conversation. So I decided to get on with my work and try to struggle through. But as time went on I found that I needed the dictionary more and more. So I got up from my desk, walked to my door and listened for sounds from the corridor. All was quiet. I gently opened the door, peeped up and down ... the coast was clear. Three steps brought me to the other student's room. I knocked as quietly as I could and listened. I heard a sound but it seemed more like a groan than a welcome. I opened the door and found the student lying on his bed and he was in pain. I approached the bed to seek the reason for his pain. He told me that he was feeling awful. I went closer, pulled down his lower eyelids and when I saw the yellow colour, I told him that he probably had the jaundice.

At that moment I heard footsteps on the corridor. I gently closed my friend's door and asked him to groan more quietly. I could hear the footsteps coming closer and closer. Suddenly the door was flung open there was the Dean. I tried to stutter out excuses about the student being ill but the only response which I received was 'To your room, Mr Doherty, to your room.' There was no argument. Again I waited for 'the visit'.

I had forgotten all about it by the time 'black Friday' had come. That was the day the entire student body gathered in the College Chapel and the President, Vice-President and all the Deans made a solemn procession through the body of the Church to the sanctuary. Then the student's names were read out and if your name was on the list, then you were being called to orders. Each student sat in his own particular seat according to his seniority in the class. We were able to watch each other during this particular exercise and when a young man's name was omitted his head went down and everyone knew that he had not been called to Orders. And so it came to my class. Some names had been jumped before it came to my row. Then my head went down ... I had not been called to Orders.

The ritual was the same for all students whose names had been omitted – report to the Dean's room next morning. And so I joined the queue. When I finally ushered into the room, my hands were perspiring and I did not feel at all well. I was harangued for breaking silences and entering another student's room and I had no defence ... I may have had reasons and excuses but they were not sought and when I tried to offer them I was told to be quiet. I was able to take all this to some extent but what I could never understand was the accusation which the Dean levelled at me when he said that I was a 'menace to society.' That made me feel very angry but prudence prevailed and I waited until I was safely outside before emitting a mighty scream. I suppose other students suffered worse ... maybe even expelled for breaking some rules.

It would be too easy for me now to sit in judgement on those days in seminary and, while the letter of the law seemed to have more importance than the law and its meaning, I honestly believe that I have many more happy memories than unhappy ones. Bonds of friendship and comraderie were formed between fellow diocesans and classmates which last not only for the duration of seminary training but afterwards into priesthood. Unfortunately for me, the other seven students from Derry who joined with me left during their time of training and although I do not see them often, I feel that we could be very much at ease in each other's company.

While our Spiritual Directors spoke to us each week on the spiritual life of the priest, the Dean also spoke to us regularly. One of his regular themes was the 'danger of particular friendships' and he was referring not only to such a friendship with a female which could develop during vacation, but he also warned us against developing such friendships with students. I would have preferred that he would have used the term 'homosexuality' if that is what he meant. As it was friendships developed naturally and I am glad to say that I have some very close friends among my own classmates which have lasted to this day.

There was some tremendous fun at College. Football was a great outlet for the students, and while I never commanded a place on either class team or the diocesan soccer team, I played for the reserves and never missed an opportunity for a 'friendly' match. My support was very vocal, especially on final-day. I still can remember one particular match and Derry was playing. I disagreed loudly and voraciously with some of the referee's decisions, so much so that the referee stopped the match and came up to me to say that, if he had to take any more abuse from me, he would have no option but to send me away from the pitch altogether. My language improved (and the bad word at Maynooth was 'feck') and my cheering continued. Derry won the match!

Drama was another popular outlet for the students. We were very privileged as one of the Abbey Players would come into the College to produce some of the plays. I had a one-liner walk-on part in a play about Galileo. I had only three words to say: 'He is dead.' I've heard great actors say that such a part in a play is most difficult... but I had better say that I was not good enough for anything more. And while in my priesthood I have discovered a talent for producing concerts and shows, I still know that I cannot act.

I think it would be true to say that most students, if not all, enter a seminary as rather immature young men (sadly many leave almost as immature). There are opportunities for developing one's talents and abilities. I was shy and somewhat backward in spite of my vocal support at soccer matches. In the early years I never gave much thought to public speaking and in college I avoided it if at all possible. My first breakthrough in this particular arena came one night when the first two years gathered in a large hall for entertainment. On that night we were to provide our own. Part of the night was given over to 'fun talk'. All the names of the students were placed in a hat (almost 200) and in another hat there were strange and funny titles. A student's name was pulled out of one hat and the title of a subject was pulled from another. The unfortunate student had then to stand up and speak impromtu for two minutes on the subject. As we laughed at the fellows struggling and stuttering and eventually failing with laughter, we waited for the next sacrifical lamb. It was me. 'Mr James Doherty, Derry' was the name called in the hall. I stood up and could feel my legs shaking. 'And your subject is 'changing nappies'.' The howl of laughter gave me a few moments to think. At that stage in my career I had five little nieces and I had changed many a nappy. So I began to share with them the benefits of my experience. A small bell rang after two minutes but it needed the outburst of applause for me to realise that my time was up. That night went a long way to clearing my shyness about public speaking and I know of several persons today who would regret that night. While I may discipline myself on a Sunday morning to keep my sermon to within five or six minutes, I can still get carried away if I were offered a microphone at an informal gathering. Offering thanks after a concert could take anything up to fifteen minutes.

Things were not all right in Maynooth in the sixties but the men of the thirties and forties thought the system in my time was rather lax. And it would be probably true to say that the students of the eighties would regard my system as rather austere and 'Colditz-like'. Today's student can have his own coffee or tea making equipment in his room; possess a radio; have a shelf-full of novels and easy access to a telephone. Whether it makes the young student today better prepared for the pastoral ministry is open to debate. Learning to mature and grow is not necessarily related to external freedom ... I believe it has more to do with the internal condition of the person. Being human involves being open to relatedness; being able to reach out to and receive from another.

The Training

In my time religious practice was compulsory. One was obliged to be present at morning Mass, unless one was excused for a very genuine reason. Other duties were incorporated into the daily timetable. These included morning meditation, a daily visit to the Blessed Sacrament, one half-hour spiritual reading in the chapel and night prayer. There were two preached retreats in the year as well as particular days of recollection. Most students accepted these duties without question. This is not to say that we looked forward to them with eager anticipation. I remember one very cold winter returning to the college after a short Christmas vacation. The heating had broken down in my block of flats. There was six inches of snow on the ground. It was a terrible struggle trying to light up a cigarette sheltering behind a large oak-tree – and a shame having to throw it away after a few long drags because of the bitter cold.

It must seem strange now, because it even seems strange to me, to think that we accepted those conditions as a matter of fact. I have a memory of going to my room at study-time and instead of removing my soutane at my desk, I put on an extra coat and scarf, pulled on my gloves and covered my head with a cap. I certainly did not study much, as I was too busy trying to keep the blood circulating round my body. If one was lucky enough to catch influenza, one could look forward to nice warm comfortable surroundings in the infirmary where the good Sisters fed you well and made sure there was heat in the sick-room.

We had a class-lecture system and again it was obligatory to attend. There was the usual pressure as would be experienced by any university student. The philosophy studies were strange to say the least but we were assured the scholastic philosophy was necessary for future studies in theology. While there are many times during the seven years' preparation that a student must sit

24

and wonder about his reasons for remaining in the college, the year of one's degree certainly helped to crystallise the choices. It was not unknown for a greater number of students than usual to decide to leave after having received their degrees and seek a different type of vocation. We, who remained behind to continue with theological studies, always felt great admiration for those who left, knowing that it was a major decision which they took and demanded some strength and maturity. And, thank God, Irish society was changing in those days and a young man could return home without a cloud of failure hanging over his head. But it also meant that we who remained in the college had a new decision. Young people often ask me and other priests, 'Why did you decide to become a priest?' and I find myself saying that it is the result of many little decisions made along the way. Why do these particular men marry these particular women ... probably after many little decisions. But it is not the purpose of this book to discuss the intricacies of relationships. It is sufficient here to say that after I received my degree I made a further decision to continue the theological course and to try to discern the purpose of my life. There were several occasions during my training that I felt urged to give more serious consideration to my main reason for being there – to become a priest. Doubts do not destroy faith; in fact they often help to purify and strengthen it. I remember going through a particularly difficult patch ... will I go or will I stay? ... have I got what it takes? ... what does it take? ... will I be able to persevere? ... am I good enough? I was reading a lot of 'spiritual books'; I was spending long hours in prayer. It was almost as if I wanted God to give me a special directive and then everything would be alright.

I discovered among my books a pastoral letter written by Pope Pius XII on the priesthood. He outlined among other things three qualities which a young man should have if he was considering the priesthood: average intelligence, average health, and a right attitude with good morals. That actually helped me at the time even though I still had to question myself about my attitude and my morals. I am probably paraphrasing now as I am working from memory, but I do believe every student gives very serious thought to his decision to remain studying for the priesthood...

just as every man and woman give very serious thought to their decision to marry.

One of the things which I now think was missing from the training is that we were not taught about prayer itself. We had times for prayer, we were given talks on prayer, we had books to read about prayer but I cannot remember being led into prayer. I used to watch my own classmates, especially at Mass after receiving the Eucharist, kneeling down and placing their hands over their faces and wondering what was going on in their heads and their hearts. Did they have as many distractions as me? Were their minds wandering off to far distant places? Did they have special words to say by which they could communicate with God himself? I do not want to blame the system here (I probably could have asked my spiritual director) but would that have been seen as doubts about my faith which a young student should not have? My own few close friends assured me that I was quite normal. So I persevered until the end, trusting more in God's grace than in my own self.

I found that I began to accept college life as normal and, in spite of the stringent regulations, I was able to get through each day. But when I went home for my vacations, I felt I had to re-adjust to the 'outside life'. It was almost like a minor culture-shock each time I went home. People did not wear black and white. Clothes were of many different colours, and, to quote a very popular song, 'there is absolutely nothing like the frame of a dame'! If you ever spend six months in the company of men only you will understand how pleasant a sight it is to see a woman. And I am not talking here about what would be called 'lustful thoughts' ... women are naturally very attractive to men and (student) priests are men.

And there is no doubt that a woman smells more beautifully. I could not get over the many types of perfume whose aromas seemed to fill the air ... and I am not saying that the students did not keep themselves clean, but men do have a certain type of B.O. and one does learn to grow accustomed to it. Having four sisters, I knew the minute I set foot inside my home that there was a fresh smell about. This too is part of the decision-making. Going home and relating with girls and deciding that I did not want to become deeply involved with any particular one. Decision has to do with choices and if I were choosing priesthood I was excluding the possibility of marriage. It can be argued that if I did not have a close relationship with a girl then I was not really making a choice. But if I had had a close relationship with a girl would I have been making a choice against the priesthood ... or would I have been free to make such a choice? I presume this point could be open to many arguments and I am sure that I have not covered all the intricate aspects of decision-making and choices.

Many of the theological lectures were fascinating and extremely interesting; others were boring, difficult and very dull. Some of this was due to the nature of the subject and some to the nature of the lecturing professor.

But looking back in hindsight I wonder did the college authorities have a definite idea of what a priest should be. Did they have a picture of a niche into which they felt they had to mould the students? And if a particular student did not fit into this niche, did they see it as their obligation to knock a few chips off him so that he could fit? And if so, were they neglecting to recognise his own special humanity? And did students unwittingly shape themselves into this imaginary niche in order to survive and thereby fail to honour their own unique selves? How many compromises can a person make without doing damage to his person? And if the authorities had this 'niche-idea' of what a priest should be, from where did they get it, considering that few of them had spent much time in parish settings? But then, pastoral theology was not even a subject in the early sixties.

Another great lacuna was the fact that there was no work done on personal development, in understanding how the person works, in enabling a young man to take himself on and discover his weak points, as well as affirming his strong qualities. Perhaps a permanent psychologist, who would give lectures as well as personal counselling, would be a useful asset to a seminary. This would be helpful not only to the student in his training days but would be of practical help to his pastoral ministry. It is foolish to assume that every person matures naturally into full manhood. There is an old adage that grace builds on nature, but if a young man is carrying scars from childhood, then grace is being laid on a very insecure foundation.

The young student too has got a very limited notion of what the finished product, the priest, is like … and that is based on his knowledge of priests that he knows. The priests whom I had known from my parish and grammar school were good men, dedicated workers and I had a definite admiration for them. But I cannot say that I liked all of them. In fact I did not really know them as men. They never seemed to be able to come out from behind their uniform. I was an altar-boy for a number of years and I remember thinking it strange that one of the priests who accompanied us on the altar-boys' excursion actually smoked. And to see him running up and down the beach as he refereed the football match was a very pleasant sight … but he did not even take off his collar. As a young boy I probably would have been shocked if he had removed the collar. The black-suit uniform was so traditional that one could not see beyond it. The standing joke was always told about the priest who 'took off his collar' to a man who challenged him to a fight … but the challenger always backed down as soon as he had 'defrocked' the priest and he was then shamed into abandoning the battle. Such things were never imagined at college. We were being taught theology in order to be able to handle confessional matters with a certain aplomb, to be able to speak with a little authority on the Scriptures, to confer the sacraments with efficiency and validity, to say (pray) the Breviary and above all to say Mass. I had been taught the Tridentine Mass in the early months of 1967 and still remember with some humour practising the making of several crosses over the wooden chalice which was part of my training equipment. And a week before ordination I was given a dispensation to practice with real wine as I was a pioneer … I still have not grown accustomed to the taste of altar-wine. It was presumed that after seven years a man was spiritually prepared not only for ordination but also for his own personal spiritual life as a priest.

I am fairly convinced that while a young man may be intellectually prepared for priesthood, he only begins to learn what is fully involved in being a priest by actually being one within a parish setting. No matter how well prepared a couple may be for marriage, they only come to a full realisation of their new state in life by being married. Hopefully young priests have as much understanding about their new role in life as do young couples have about theirs.

The Spring

Most young priests have what may be euphemistically called a 'honeymoon period'. My ordination day was blessed with beautiful weather and I stepped out into brilliant sunshine to be greeted by my parents, family and friends. The men with whom I had been ordained, men that I had played football with, exchanged a few poker hands, shared a cigarette stub, were smiling embarrassedly as people knelt before them for the 'first blessing'. We shared blessings among ourselves and felt a tinge of sadness that after seven years of living together as brothers and friends that we were now going our separate ways. And yet we were unable to share this together. The handshakes were tight and masculine, the good wishes were sincere, the smiles were broad and the eyes were dry. There was the real hope that we would keep in contact but probably the greater realisation was that we were really saying goodbye. After the ordination meal I joined my family for the long run home to Derry. I sat in my first present – a second-hand Morris Minor – along with my parents and one of my brothers. My car led a small cavalcade of about six cars. They joked about calling me 'Father Doherty' as we made the slow journey northwards. It is impossible to keep a small group of six cars together if you travel more than 20 m.p.h. and so we had to stop in Strabane to tighten ranks. I wanted to go on ahead but when my mother advised me to allow my brother to drive and that I should sit in the front passenger seat, I began to wonder what she had planned. It wasn't until we were two miles from Derry that my mother finally told me that the neighbours would be waiting to greet me. I could not believe there were so many people living in so few streets. It is a pity there were no video cameras then because it would have been captured on camera that I was totally dumbstruck and overcome with the sense of joy and pride written all over the people's faces. I think that they too shared in the fact that one of their own, a young man from a working-class family, was now within the ranks of the priesthood. And I was proud of them too. I scrambled into my home and collapsed on the sofa and as I sat there trying to recover from the surprise and shock, my mother again advised me that I should go into the street and greet the people who were waiting for my blessing. The local Administrator was also there to welcome me and he supported my mother's wishes. He is a priest who always had my respect and admiration, a man of gentleness and even shyness, and with such encouragement, I ventured out to the doorway. I was able to muster up a few words and when I gave the people my blessing, I moved down to be among them. The honeymoon had begun.

As I explained in my previous book, *It's never the same*, I had to wait until October for my first appointment. I had no real definite sense of ministry; I just wanted to be with people and serve them as best I could. And for me it was a 24-hour, 7-day-a-week service. I now had two rooms to myself and shared a common dining-room. The parish priest was in his late sixties, two curates in their mid-fifties and a curate in his mid-forties. I can say now that I was blessed with such company. At the time I felt that I was a young boy all over again. But they treated me as one of the team and gave me practical advice that one could not find in a theological manual or text book. They warned me about the 'con-men' who would want to take advantage of a young green curate. It took me some time to be able to distinguish between the genuine cases and the bluffers but I also got to admire in a funny sort of way the craft and ingenuity of the con-artist. There was real comradeship among the priests and I never met men with so many funny stories. A Saturday night became a sort of social night. People sometimes wonder about a priest after he hears confessions. When I first began hearing confessions, the practice was to sit in a closed box from six o' clock until ten o' clock. And even in the late sixties one could be kept busy for the four hours. Upon leaving the box, I was tired, my eyes felt tight, my legs were numb and I just wanted to walk up and down in the senior curate's room to watch *Match of the Day*. After verifying the order of Masses for the next day, it was bedtime.

Shortly after I had arrived there, I was informed that I was to be deacon at a High Mass. I joined the parish priest and the senior curate in the sacristry for vesting. Everything was going alright until we had vested up to the chasuble. Then the two older men reached for their birettas. They looked at me and asked where was my biretta. I informed then that I had none and wondered was this going to be my first row. But again age has its own wisdom. The Parish Priest said that it would look rather funny with birettas on two men and the third without one, so the simple solution was for all to go 'headless'. In its own little way it was a big decision for men who had consistently worn birettas for many years to go without them. So instead of a row, it became a joke. To the outsider it probably was more a matter of common sense. But at a deeper level there was the question of relationship. I felt I had been respected and I respected them for giving me so much space. I could have been ordered to borrow a biretta and 'made' to wear it.

I am still amazed at the trust placed in a priest. I assumed that people with big problems would have gone to the older and wiser men but within a very short time men and women who could have been my parents were coming to me for advice and counsel. This is a truly humbling experience. My mother used ask me how I was getting on and I was very reluctant to speak about any of my work as I regarded it as being very confidential. My mother respected this and did not wish to know who or what I was dealing with ... she merely was interested in my happiness and wanted to offer me support.

When I told her that I was speaking at a pre-marriage course, her only response was 'What do you know about marriage?' And when I replied that I was one of the products of her marriage and I had three brothers and three sisters married and so I might be able to say a few things to prospective couples, she simply grunted and said, 'I suppose that means I could talk to some priests about priesthood.' And she probably could. I soon learned that priests are in a very privileged position. I was chaplain to a psychiatric hospital for nine years. I tried to visit the short-term patients at least once a week. I was on my usual rounds one particular day and found myself sitting by the bedside of an elderly lady. She began to tell me her sad and sore story. I listened as well as I could and then, when she mentioned a very specific point, I asked her what the doctors had advised her about it. She said to me with great firmness, 'O, father, I wouldn't tell the doctor that!' It took me some time to persuade her to inform the doctor about what she had told me as I felt it was very relevant to her sickness.

Then there was the night that I was called to the main general hospital at three o' clock in the morning. It was my first emergency sick-call and as I drove to the hospital I was trying to clear the sleep from my eyes. I approached the casualty entrance and went through the doors. A hospital at night must be as quiet as a convent. My footsteps made such loud echoes that I decided to walk on my tip-toes. Suddenly a young nurse appeared from a room. She took one look at me and said gently, 'You must be new, father.' 'Yes', I said, 'this is my first call.' 'Well', she said, 'there is an old lady here, father, who fell down her stairs and is dead.' Then she led me into a room and there was a stretcher with a body on it. The body's face was covered with a towel and I could see the blood seeping through it. I was totally at a loss. Our training had instructed us to anoint the forehead of a person in an emergency situation. The nurse seemed to realise my dilemma without my having to say a word. 'It would not be a pretty sight, father, so you may anoint her hand,' said the nurse as she held up the lady's hand to anoint. I thanked her for her kindness and returned to my car. I drove back more slowly and although I went back to bed, I got very little sleep that night.

Again when I told my fellow priests the next day they were very supportive and told me that I needed to expect such situations in the hospital and that time and experience would surely break me in and enable me to cope. I felt that they understood and they did not try to make me feel small. I was learning. Many similar situations did arise and I found that as well as receiving the support of the priests, the sisters and nurses were very considerate. I suppose these are things that could not be taught in a seminary situation and life becomes its own teacher. And while I was growing in confidence, I was also becoming aware of how much I did not know. The theories which I had been taught from manuals now had to be applied to real life situations. The hospital threw up many of the moral dilemmas which until then were mere abstract theorising ... abortion, ectopic pregnancies, sterilisation, hysterectomy ... and they concerned mostly women. While there may be apparent black-and-white answers in the text-books, it never was as simple as that when you were face to face with a human person struggling with the problem. I would not want to give the impression that a young priest has to carry heavy burdens all the time. There were many fun moments for the young priest, and I found this out when I began to visit the primary schools.

I always loved children and I found that I could sit and chat with school children for hours. They made me feel very welcome ... I suppose anything was better than formal class for them. And they also educated me. Their young minds were still open and their questions and answers were novel and sometimes illuminating. I remember speaking to a group of little girls, aged about eight, about purgatory as we approached November. I asked them why souls stayed in purgatory and a little girl replied, 'Because there are not enough beds in heaven.' And the little boy who told me that the Catholic Church was way ahead in the space-race. When I asked him to explain, he walked up to the front of the class and with great confidence lifted a piece of chalk and drew a coffin on the blackboard and said, 'There, father, that takes you straight to heaven.'

When I was fit and well I used love visiting homes and meeting the families. On one such occasion, I was in a home with a mother surrounded by her six children. One of the little girls wanted to make a cup of tea. Within minutes the tea was presented to me on a tray. But when I took the first sip of the tea, I knew there was something wrong. The mother noticed the grimace on my face and asked me what was wrong. I smiled and said that I thought salt had been put in the cup instead of sugar. We were all able to laugh about it and I made sure to return to the house in case they thought I might have been offended. I also learned to be careful about indicating certain preferences. In one home, the mother asked me if I liked fig-rolls. I told her they were one of my favourite biscuits. Well, I got fig-rolls in every house on that street as the news was spread. For me, house visitation was very important and while it was a great way to get to know your people, it could become a difficult task. As trust was built up between myself and the people, I found myself being drawn into many personal problems – a pregnant daughter, a marriage that was beginning to experience relationship difficulties, a young boy or man who had become involved in the political and civil unrest. All of these cases and others similar to them would eat up my time as I tried to be available to listen, advise or counsel.

What I was not really prepared for was the belligerent, irrational and angry person. What was I to do with my anger? Was it wrong for me to feel angry? Does one take abuse whether warranted or not and pretend that one is not upset? These moments were rare but real. It was just as difficult to deal with the adulation expressed when one said 'a lovely Mass'. I remember myself being surrounded by a hundred screaming children, everyone of them vieing with one another to hold my hand. I suppose I was a bit different from the other priests who had long since passed that stage. Even the clothes which I wore were different. I had purchased a leather jacket because I could not afford to buy a new black suit every six months. I had also invested in an anorak which had a few bright colours dappled through it. The parish priest smiled at my dress and called me 'the anorak kid.' Within a few years a few other younger men joined the parish and then the black suit became the Sunday dress.

What did cause a few raised eyebrows was the fact that teenagers began to favour my company and would actually visit the parochial house socially. This was a little unknown. The parochial house was the home of the priests and it had two rooms in which callers could be seen for business. I can see now that it was a bit unfair of me to have young boys and girls traipsing through the corridors of a shared house. What may have been more serious was my need to be liked, to be approved of, to be seen to be serving. In what way was I trying to live up to the notion of the priest who is always on call, always available, to whom nothing was a problem? There were certainly some overtones of the 'Messiah complex' as well as the young man needing to be successful. I found myself responding to any and every need, wanting to please, wanting to solve problems, even believing I had the answers. I must have been a terrible headache for the older priests ... but full credit to them, they never offered a word of criticism. Occasionally they would tell me to ease up, to take time out, to take a break. But it was my springtime and I was bubbling over ... and I was naïve.

Two things happened that caused me to stand back a little and observe. First of all I became ill and secondly a few younger men joined the team. New questions began to surface ... what vision of priesthood was I working out of? What is priesthood in a busy urbanised parish? What time was I giving to my own personal prayer? What time was I giving to myself? Are there different visions of priesthood? Spring-time means digging up the soil and turning it as well as admiring the pretty flowers. I was beginning to form the questions but where could I find the answers?

Some of these questions seemed a bit esoteric when I began to hear the stories of other young priests. I began to realise that my own situation had many blessings when I discovered what was regarded as normal in other situations. I was quite amazed when a young curate told me that his 'day-off' began after the ten o' clock Mass in the morning and if it happened to be a funeral Mass, then he would not be able to get away until midday, and he was to report back to the parochial house at 10 p.m. that same evening. He was not allowed visitors into the house and if he was leaving the parish boundaries other than on his day-off, he had to inform his parish priest where he was going and the nature of the meeting. Sometimes people wonder why there may be two or three parochial houses in a rural parish. There may be historical reasons initially so that a priest may not be too far away from his people, especially before modern transport and easy communication by telephone. Certainly it would be financially cheaper to live together in the one house, but a parish priest and a curate might not be able to live together. And this is not always the fault of the older man. Young men too have their own idiosyncracies and the chemistry of the two men might not blend. This might surprise some people who would say that priests should be able to relate positively and overcome their little differences. But priests are only men with all the human failings of other men. Sometimes the parish priest 'lords' it over his curate as well as his people. There can be some situations where the two priests do not even talk together and the parish priest passes on instructions by way of notes left on the dining-room table or slipped under the curate's bedroom door. There have been times when the curate learned about renovation work being done to the Church only when the workmen arrived. And it is very sad for a curate to learn about parish work from his parishioners or the housekeeper. The parish priest does not have to consult with his curate but it would seem fair and proper if he did. And I believe the same obligation rests on the curate. He may have left his seminary training full of innovative ideas but he would be a foolish man if he began to establish groupings within the parish without at least informing his parish priest.

For too long we have all been caught up in the 'permission-sought-permission-given' syndrome. Without going into lengthy and deep discussions about parish vision, surely two grown men should be able to sit down and talk through their ideas. It is rarely a different theological view that separates two priests. Possibly they may be working out of different models of Church. But even this could be open for sharing and understanding. There are very human factors involved here. If a man has been working in a particular way for thirty years, he is obviously going to find it very difficult to change. The problem increases when he refuses the younger priest to initiate what are very commendable changes. It can be very frustrating for the young priest who advises the introduction of lay-readers or extraordinary eucharistic ministers to be told by the parish priest that 'those new-fangled things will not be implemented in my parish.' And it is not unknown for the parish priest to defend his position by saying that the people do not want them, irrespective of whether the people have been consulted or not. While recourse may be made to the bishop, he can be left in an invidious position. It would not make a bishop's life any easier if he were to 'interfere' in the internal workings of a parish. The bishop has to trust the man whom he has invested with the running of the parish. And yet it may be dangerous to allow the young priest to fester with his frustrations. In many ways the younger man may have to work out compromises as it should be easier for him to cope than it would be for the older man to change.

I want to make it clear that I am not pointing the finger at any particular person. I have been in the position of curate and Administrator and I believe I am able to give a view for both sides. I do not think it is merely a question of authority and obedience. It is a more basic and human question of being able to listen to each other, to question each other and to work together as brothers. But it has to be recognised that some personalities simply do not mix. It would be very foolish of the younger man to disregard the experience of his elder ... and it would be very foolish of the older man not to listen to what the younger man has to say. Each has a lot to learn from the other but the ability to listen is not something that is taught in a lecture hall ... nor is it given with the Sacrament of Orders.

Often the young priest is too busy learning the ropes of the parish and the implications of his ministry so that, in spite of his frustration, he does not have time to sit and ponder over it. I think it is to the credit of many a young priest that he is more than anxious to 'practise his trade.' If he is at all involved with his work, he will find his hours eaten away by all sorts of calls ... and by being drawn into the lives of his people, he will learn to grow and develop. And yet it is not unknown for the new parish priest to prefer to stay in his room hiding behind the comfort of his books. He may find it difficult to relate with people. Gone are the days when the priest's word is the last word on the subject. Both young and old priests have to cope with this development. I believe it is a more healthy way of being; but it too can be pushed to its limits and the word or comment of the priest is regarded as totally irrelevant.

But springtime is springtime and the young priest soon learns to cope with day to day situations. I know that I loved every blessed and cursed moment of it. And I was particularly blessed by the priest-friends whom I had found. We came together out of a similar need ... in the midst of busy days and heavy pastoral problems, we began to sense our own particular need for God. We may have been involved in helping to build his kingdom ... but it seemed imperative that we become involved personally with him. So a small group of us came together to support each other in this quest. We never realised what it would lead to. We first thought that we would meet in each others' parochial houses but that soon proved to be impractical because the man of the house was sure to be called to the door or the telephone several times in the day; and it was a bit unfair on the housekeeper to say that there would be four or five extra for lunch. It took us the best part of a year to settle on the quiet of a Good Shepherd Convent, where we could have the privacy of a room, the availability of the chapel, a couple of cups of coffee spread throughout the day and a good meal at midday ... for which we paid. The payment was our decision and I dread to think how callous we might have been if we expected such hospitality *gratis*. After meeting for some time we heard about the Jesus-Caritas Fraternity groupings and we tried to model our gathering on them.

It became a tremendous support for prayer and a forum for open and honest discussion. There are many different forms of prayer today and one may find people and priests arguing for or against particular types. I believe that people will be drawn to whatever form suits them and I believe that people will be very loathe to canonise any special one. I found that I was being attracted to the silent, contemplative form of prayer ... and it was not a question of 'first love'. My prayer life had become whittled down to Mass, the breviary and the occasional rosary but so much of it was 'duty-stuff'! I believed in God but he was Almighty, Omnipotent, Creator. And I have to admit that it is quite difficult to form a personal relationship with such a being. So when we gathered for our meetings, we would share about our experience of prayer ... my usual response was that it was dry, dull, difficult and short. We had decided that we would try to give God some personal time apart from our 'duty-prayers'. I used to be amazed when I listened to my brother-priests when they spoke of spending from half an hour to an hour in such quiet prayer – we would not dare be so presumptuous – but we merely encouraged each other to try. I got a great cheer the day that I admitted to spending fifteen minutes before the Blessed Sacrament. The gentle encouragement helped and there was no trace of competitiveness or failure or being disgraced. It was the first time that I heard priests talk openly about their prayer and their struggle with it. And it was in that setting that we began to talk about priesthood and its meaning in today's world. Sharing became easier as we learned to trust one another and to recognise the confidentiality of the grouping. There were no mind-blowing thoughts being expressed but there was a real intimacy being shared.

The meetings were to be held monthly and after almost fifteen years we are still meeting. That in itself says something about the group. There have been a few personnel changes within the group but the core of the group has remained the same. The present group has been together for about ten years but it has been reduced to six from seven because of the death of one of the members. While we all appreciate the worth of the meetings, the oldest member, who happens to be a retired parish priest, is forever lauding the existence of the group and keeps wondering how it could be spread even further. He regrets that it was not in existence in his youth and believes it will help him move into old age more gracefully ... although it has to be admitted that he is a graced person. I feel that I have been graced by this group which has given me such personal support not only in the springtime of my priesthood but throughout my growing years. It is indeed a great blessing to be able to sit with men of varying ages and discuss not only pastoral problems but also particular parish difficulties. It has been for me a great help towards personal maturity and growth. But let it be said that it is not a mutual pat on the back society. We are prepared to take one another on and disagree with expressed viewpoints and do so without falling out and remaining judgemental. Some priests may say that that can work as long as you do not have to work together in the same parish. It so happens that I have spent a number of years with four of the men in different parishes (and one of them was my curate for four years). That the same attitude does not exist in every parish is sad but also realistic. The Church institution as experienced at the local level is no more perfect than the world-wide Church institution.

The Derry priests as a grouping are as happy as any other grouping of priests. This is seen very clearly when we come together each year for our annual retreat in Ards Monastery. There is a total mixing of men coming together to pray, to concelebrate the Eucharist, to eat a common meal and to laugh and joke together at break-times. There is a real spirit of brotherhood which is particularly marked, for me at least, at confessional time. We are just like any other group of men lining up to seek forgiveness for our sins and failings. Children sometimes find this rather funny, thinking that we somehow looked into a mirror and waved the magic hand of forgiveness over ourselves. And even we wonder about how sympathetic an ear we will receive from the absolving confessor. It is good for us to go to a stranger as it helps us understand the ordinary feelings of our parishioners. Personally speaking, I prefer to go to confession to a man who knows me and my past and can offer me guidance as well as absolution. I have a great belief in the Sacrament of Reconciliation and know of its healing power with regard to my faults and weaknesses. I have a great trust in its sacredness and its seal. In spite of the human foibles of the priest, it must say something about the Sacrament of Orders that this sacrament has survived so long with the seal preserved ... definitely a proof of God's existence.

And there may lie the greatest challenge to any priest anywhere. His work touches on the very things of God and yet he himself is such a broken person. I think it was Leo Trèse who described the priest as 'a vessel of clay'. Maybe we are afraid to admit this to ourselves and our people will not let us either. I once knew a man who was the father of a very large family. He became rather ill and although he was not immediately aware of it, he was dying of cancer. I loved him deeply and enjoyed the times we spent together. He was a man of prayer and deep humility and often when we did come together he would talk of his privilege in being with me, the priest, and one whom he could call 'friend'. Our favourite chat used to arise when he would say, 'Because you are priest, father, you are on a different level from me,' and in spite of my protestations that I was just a man like himself, he would shake his head and say simply, 'Ah, but you are a priest and that is different.' I would speak to him of his great vocation as a husband and father and the dignity we both shared as baptised persons. But he would giggle softly and say, 'But a priest is different.' Theologically speaking there is a difference but he constantly made the point that I as a priest was 'higher'. We became close friends out of it all and just agreed to disagree. My service to the Church was different from his, but was it any better?

Springtime is known for its frosts and bitter sharp spells as well as its bright, healthy periods. We take the necessary precautions against the weather but there is always a sense that things are going to improve. The first sign of the early daffodils adding a bit of colour to the white snowdrops gives us a bit of hope that change is on the way. As a young priest I enjoyed each new day as it brought new challenges into my life. Young people have often said to me that a priest's life must be very boring. That reminds me of the frequent comment of the British soldier examining my driving licence at a checkpoint on a Sunday, 'Work finished for another week, father!' I am able to say that there is probably more variety and challenge in a priest's life than in any other occupation. A priest may be doing what may be regarded as mundane type of work as he signs Mass-cards, fills in passport application forms, balances his financial books, visits his parish houses, calls in to see the school-children, brings Holy Communion to the sick, and these duties are part and parcel of every priest's work. But he may be called upon to help in a marriage problem, bring comfort to a person dying of cancer, try to advise and support a young unmarried mother, give counsel to a young drug-addict, become involved with a family coping with an alcoholic parent, and these are only some of the situations which may arise any day. The priest cannot always prepare for such eventualities but when any of them does occur, the priest may find that he must give hours of his time in any week to any of these difficult and heart-breaking events. It is immediately obvious how quickly a priest will mature as he tries to work through any of these cases. He himself will need support and help in order to be able to cope. I have found not only my priest-fraternity to be of help but also the few very close priest friends with whom I have been blessed.

When one is trying to respond to the many cases which may occur at any time, it is not always easy to distinguish between the important, the urgent, the necessary. Time and experience help the young priest to discern and be able to make decisions which he can stand over. But, of course, the person who calls at the door always has the most urgent task for the priest. There was one particular day and I had just received an urgent and emergency call to the hospital. I immediately went to the Oratory to receive the pyx with the Blessed Sacrament and rushed down the stairs taking them two at a time. I ran out of the front door and jumped the four steps with one leap. At that very moment, an elderly lady appeared and shouted to me. I asked her to excuse me as I was rushing to get to the hospital. 'But this will only take a minute, father.' I hesitated, thinking it must be a Mass-card, but I stayed at my car. She approached me and began searching through her handbag ... now women's handbags are something else! My sisters used to say that they carried everything in their handbags apart from the kitchen-sink. Anyway, the lady began to rummage through papers, handkerchiefs, purses, rosary beads, loose change until she produced a document. 'It's a passport form for my son. You see, father, he works during the day and asked me to bring this down to one of the priests. You know, he got a job in Du Pont last year and he wants to take a wee holiday abroad ...' At that stage I was wondering why he could not have come himself at night after work. 'He's married now, father, and I have his wife's form here as well. She's a lovely girl ... I'm sure you know her ...' Now, where might she be, I thought. When I finally got the forms, I discovered that they lived in another parish altogether. I said nothing and managed to get the signing done on the roof of the car. As I scrambled into my car after the delay, I heard the lady say, 'I hope the sick person will be alright, father. I'll just go into the chapel and light a candle.' The person in the hospital was still alive even though unconscious, and he had been unconscious for some time so even getting to the hospital earlier would not have made much difference. When I had got back to the parochial house, I had calmed down sufficiently to be able to smile at the very human situation ... and yet it was quite a common thing to happen and whenever I heard that someone wished to see me at the door for 'just a minute,' I prepared myself for at least a ten-minute conversation.

I suppose that is one of the interesting facets of the priestly life ... one never knows what might happen from one hour to another. I was on hospital duty on a particular week and the usual routine was to visit the hospital and meet any patients who had to face an operation the next day. I was doing my rounds at a relaxed pace when I received word to report immediately to the cardiac unit. Upon arrival the sister met and apologised. 'A young man has just been admitted with a heart attack, father, but he has left instructions that he does not want to see any priests ... and he is a Catholic.' 'His wishes must be respected,' I said, 'but please keep me informed of developments.' At that very moment, alarm bells began to ring all over the place. I stood back and waited to see if I might be needed. The sister of the ward came up to me and said, 'That young man's heart has just stopped, father, and doctors are with him trying to revive him. What do you think you should do?' So many thoughts rushed through my head and I walked into the ward to see a young man in his late twenties lying on a stretcher, and doctors and nurses working ferociously with him. 'You better do what you have to do, father,' said one of the doctors, 'as we will be taking this man down to the intensive care unit.' I decided immediately. I took out the oils from my pocket and went and stood at the head of the man so as to stay out of the way of the nursing staff. I quietly anointed his forehead and whispered a few prayers into the man's ears. 'We have to go, father, sorry,' said the doctor. The stretcher was whisked away and I went in to speak to the sister. 'I'm grateful that you anointed him, father. At least he died with the blessing of God upon him.' I was not so sure that I had done what was right but I kept re-assuring myself that it would have been his last dying wish. All that I needed that night was to get back to the parochial house and get a strong cup of coffee. My fellow priests assured me that I had not done anything wrong.

I was on hospital duty the next night as well. Before leaving the hospital that night I called to see the sister from the night before. 'Well, have you got a surprise tonight, father!' she said with a smile. 'What's that?' I asked. 'That young man who "died" last night was revived and wants to see you.' I felt my legs quiver a little but asked where I could find him. I approached the ward with some little trepidation. The young man was supported up in his bed by several pillows. I pulled the screens, sat down and introduced myself. Before I could begin to make an explanation, the young man began the conversation. 'I want to thank you, father, for what you did last night and to apologise for my bad manners.' 'But I thought that I should be apologising to you ,' I said. 'No, please, father,' he said, 'do you know that I heard and saw everything last night as the doctors and nurses were trying to revive me, and I heard in particular your own prayers and I am really grateful. Now, would you mind doing me another favour? Would you hear my confession and give me Communion?' I was not very familiar in those days with what is known as a 'near death experience', but I accepted what the gentleman had to say and proceed to grant his request.

We priests live very privileged lives and I thank God for his personal support to me in those early days. I suppose only we priests know how varied our lives can be even though we can never be prepared for the unexpected.

Years pass very fast when one's time is full and often it is only upon reflection that we begin to appreciate the full depth of our experiences. Sometimes people never notice the colour in their gardens until the flowers begin to lose their petals. And young priests assimilate their knowledge and experience without giving it a complete analytical comprehension. Soon the young priest is no longer the young priest. He may begin to notice the small physical changes at first … a few more grey hairs, a few less hairs, an added wrinkle, a slightly protruding stomach and more younger priests joining the ranks. He begins moving into the middle-aged grouping of priests and begins asking at priests' retreats, 'Who is the young fellow over there?' By that time his 'summer season' has begun.

The Summer

After a number of years doing the normal pastoral work, the priest begins to look more closely at his life and possibly begins to try to assess priorities. What are the needs of this parish that are not being met? What problems does my parish share with another? Am I using my time efficiently?

One of the things about which I felt deeply was the difficulties people were experiencing in marriage. Another priest and myself were asked to investigate the possibility of establishing a branch of the Catholic Marriage Advisory Council. I thought that this would meet the needs not just of my own parish but of every parish in the Diocese. And so I assisted Fr Seamus O' Connell in making the investigation and having such a service provided for the Diocese. I had begun to realise that many couples needed more than my listening ear; they needed more professional help which would be provided by specially trained counsellors. I undertook to take the training myself and that was something I never regretted. It can be very easy to try to offer instantaneous advice to a couple who present you with a problem and fail to get to the root cause of the difficulty. I remember with some humour listening to a couple many years ago who came to me after six months into their marriage. I asked them when problems first began and when she said, 'the honeymoon,' I could feel myself getting a little bit uneasy. But I stayed with it and asked her to be a little more specific, not knowing what was going to be said. 'He squeezes the toothpaste at the centre of the tube instead of the bottom,' she said with great deliberation. They stayed with it for a number of sessions and it turned out to be a matter of giving one another their own space and that marriage required some time for two people to learn to live together and respect one another's space. I do not believe that marriage gives permission to either partner to totally invade another person's life. Kahlil Gibran speaks of there being enough space between lovers so that the breeze can blow gently through.

Priests too have to learn this message, especially if they are living in the same house. It was something which I learned to appreciate in my first parochial house. As I said, I was the youngest priest in a house of five priests. Each of us had a bedroom and sitting room and if I were in my room the other priests would knock before entering. Maybe I was still suffering from the Maynooth experience whereby the Dean would knock, open the door immediately and be at my desk within two seconds. Of course I was receiving the message to do likewise when approaching another priest's room. This is common practice with priests who live together and it is a very practical arrangement. This is not to say that there is not quite a lot of socialising done among priests themselves ... and there can be some fun and laughter and a few practical jokes.

When I was Adminstrator in St Mary's, Creggan, I had just come in from confessions and gone to my room. It was my birthday and I had my cards placed along the mantle-piece. I sat down to watch the television when the intercom system buzzed on my telephone. I lifted the receiver and the housekeeper sounded somewhat distraught when she told me that a drunken man was in the call-room and refused to leave. I volunteered to look after the matter. When I entered the call-room I saw a figure lying on the floor dressed in a shabby-looking coat and wearing a dishevelled cap. I called out to him to get up but he simply groaned and let an empty guinness bottle fall from his hand. I called out again and asked his name. But there was no intelligible response. I went over to him and tried to get him up to a sitting position. Then his cap fell off and he turned to me and laughed with great glee ... it was one of my curates. I still did not understand the meaning of the joke until I returned to my sitting-room and there were the rest of the curates with the two housekeepers sitting around my coffee table and neatly placed upon it was a birthday cake with candles lit and burning. The party lasted a few hours filled with song, stories and laughter.

When a priest has spent a few years in a parish, he makes many friends. There are a number of families who make him feel very welcome and who treat him almost as one of the family ... a home where he can throw off his shoes and even help in making a cup of tea. It is by means of visitation that a priest truly gets to know his people and it is a very useful way of helping him to prepare his sermons. If a sermon is to be effective it must be related to the lives of the people. A priest is called to translate the words of Scripture to the everyday life of the parishioner. And I know it can be a very difficult task. Not all priests are good speakers but that does not make them bad priests. His most effective sermon is the life which he leads himself and the way in which he relates with his people. But it is amazing and even frightening how people will judge a Mass by the sermon itself. I have often asked young people how they experience the Sunday Mass and invariably they will say it was very boring. If I push them on what they mean by that statement, the typical answer is 'the sermon was very dull and had nothing to say to us'.

A very good way of trying to understand this is for the priest to visit a Sunday Mass in a parish where he is not known (and, of course, in 'civvies'). At this moment in time I am on a break in order to rest up because of an exacerbation in my diseased condition. I attended the Sunday Mass in the local church. It was a young priest who happened to be saying the Mass. The tone of his voice was monotonous and unvaried and he chose as the theme of his sermon the 'covenant relationship' between God and his people. From a theological point of view, he was quite orthodox, but as time went on it was obvious to me that the people were not with him. Maybe it was one of his poorer days and I certainly would not want to pass judgement on just one hearing. I'm sure I have bored people out of their minds on many occasions.

Writing a sermon is not an easy task. How does one speak to a congregation of people whose ages range from two to eighty-two? And to be fair to my fellow-priests I know that most of them take considerable time in preparing their Sunday talk. I'm not sure that priests fully realise how blessed they are. What other group of men have an audience in front of them every week? ... a group of people who actually want to listen and who will listen if we direct our thoughts and words to them? As well as that the priest may be faced with the same congregation every Sunday and no matter how gifted he may be, it is very difficult to be able to say something new on every single occasion. It is certainly a mighty challenge to the preacher ... to be topical, to be conversational, to be captive, to be Scriptural, to be communicative. Some priests whom I know struggle for hours to get those few words ready, reading the Scripture of the Sunday, trying to understand it for himself, consulting commentaries, reading homily notes in various magazines and then putting all of this into words which are intelligible for their people. I remember the words of Canon McGarry, who was a professor of homiletics in Maynooth and who has since died, 'If you do not strike oil in the first three minutes, stop boring!'

I am afraid that priests are not the best storytellers and we have lost the knack of using stories to illustrate a point. We seem to favour moralising and giving what I call 'salad' sermons ... 'let us ... (lettuce).' One of the most popular words in many a priest's sermon is the word 'should'. So many priests feel it is their obligation and duty to get their people into heaven. I once heard an elderly priest who had been left alone in his parish for three days when his curates were away, saying, 'Do you know that I was responsible for 3,000 souls while you were off enjoying yourselves?' The sad thing is that he might have believed that.

And there is the point which few people might be fully aware of, that the priest might be nervous as he stands in front of several hundred people. Experience may help him to control his nerves but it may not help him to be always relaxed. I remember saying my first Mass in a new parish. There were almost nine hundred people packed into the Church, the main choir was singing the entrance hymn with the full backing of a large pipe-organ. I proceeded to the small lectern for the opening greeting of the Mass and, while the choir was harmonising its way through the various verses, I was looking down at many new and strange faces. What goes on in the minds of people as they look up at their 'new priest'... 'Does he say a 'fast' Mass? what age is he? why did the

Bishop have to change my predecessor?' Their faces did not reveal what was going on in their minds. My eyes gradually came to focus on a little girl with red curling hair who was standing in the very front row. Her eyes caught mine and with the beauty and innocence that only a child possesses, she smiled up and gave me a mighty wink with her eye. I returned the welcome and we smiled at each other. I found myself relaxing completely and felt at home. I doubt if anyone even noticed the wink but they may have noticed my immediate composure.

I still write out my sermons even after twenty-four years in the ministry. I carry my notes to the ambo, but make it a point never to read them. They help to give me a start, hold me to the point and tell me when to finish. I look at my people as I preach and am able to know if they are listening. I have enough experience to stop short if I feel that I am losing them, because there is nothing worse than a priest babbling on with nothing to say, yet believing he has to spend the six or seven minutes at his job. By writing out my sermon I am at least treating it as a serious matter which I believe it is. And it would be foolish of me or any priest to think that he is going to deliver startling words of wisdom each time he preaches. Again the Sacrament of Ordination does not bestow a gift of oratory on any man. But I also believe in God's Holy Spirit present in that assembly and opening up people's hearts to his word. People sometimes say that the 'magic and mystery' have gone from the vernacular Mass and they hanker back to the old Latin Mass. I can understand what they mean by that statement but I have such a strong faith in the Eucharist that I find the mystery of each Mass still pulls at my mind and heart. That Jesus Christ would be willing to take over a little piece of bread and a few drops of wine is a mystery that challenges every fibre of my being ... and that he would do this in order to be my food and life. The Mass was not translated into English so that I or anybody could understand it, but rather that it might be a help for all of us to participate more fully in the Sacrament who is Christ.

While people may talk about being bored with some of the liturgical services, I think it is true to say that priests can experience a certain boredom too. After several years in the ministry, the priest has to fight his own sense of the mundane. One of the things that can bring this on is the celebration of marriage. Working in a busy parish, a priest may be asked to officiate at many marriage celebrations. I actually have a special fondness for the liturgical celebration of marriage itself and I am continually enthused by witnessing to two young people committing themselves to each other for life. It can only be love that can motivate such self-giving and sacrifice, the same motivating qualities which initially draws a young man to the priesthood. Their commitment encourages me in my own commitment. But as well as witnessing to their vows being expressed at Mass, then the priest is expected to attend the wedding reception with the young couple and their families. Everybody is usually in great form and looking forward to the meal and celebrations. A priest may have to be present at approximately forty or fifty such gatherings in the year ... listening to the same stories, eating the same meals, laughing at the same jokes. The majority of weddings take place on Saturdays and so when the speeches are over, the priest will have to be back in the parish to hear confessions. It is tiring, but refusing to go may be taken as an insult. I know priests who thoroughly enjoy such occasions and would even try to fit in two in the same day. Because of my present sickness, I am usually so exhausted after the Church service that I have to go to rest immediately afterwards and so am unable to get to many wedding receptions. And as I am not attached as a curate to a particular parish, I am rarely requested to officiate at marriages. It actually means that I enjoy the few to which I am asked now. By the way, I would gladly swop my sickness for a hundred weddings in the year!

Another very difficult task for the priest is the saying of funeral Masses. Again a priest may find that he is saying requiem Masses two or three times each week. I once had eight funerals in the same week. The difficulty here is not boredom; in a sense it is the problem of sensitivity. There are very few original statements that a priest can make at the Mass and he wants to be able to say something to the grieving family that will give them some support. Of course there will be many occasions while visiting the bereaved family where the priest can offer most support and comfort. These are very special opportunities for the priest and it would be a pity if he missed out on them through carelessness or insensitivity. Many a family carries deep hurts because of the poor attitude of priests on these occasions. And there is nothing a family remembers more than the kind word and visit from the priest at a death.

There are a few dangers which a priest must try to avoid ... and I say this out of sad experience on my own part and that of my fellow-priests. We can too easily fall back on pious platitudes and cliched 'holy words'. 'It's God's will' is the favourite one no matter how we try to dress it up ... but that might be the last thing a mother wants to hear on the death of her husband, and little children will wonder what sort of a God it is who would take their father when they needed him. Furthermore the family may be struggling to deal with a lot of mixed-up emotions and the 'platitudinous' priest may just be the wrong medicine.

I remember being called to a house to attend a man who had just dropped dead in the sitting-room. The fact that he had a weak heart did not make it any easier for his wife and children. After I had anointed him and sat with the wife as she told me the story of his last dying minutes, I rose to leave and the wife called me back and asked me to call on her married daughter who lived a few doors away. I readily agreed and the mother offered to show me the way and introduce me. As we walked up the street, the mother said that the daughter was in a terrible state and might need the doctor. The mother opened the door and walked in in front of me. Sitting by the fireside sobbing very loudly was the daughter. 'Here's the priest to see you,' said the mother. The face, reddened by tears, turned to anger as the daughter rose slowly, reached for the Sacred Heart picture above the mantle-piece and threw it violently at me as she cursed the God who took her father. The picture missed me (thankfully) and while the young girl's husband grabbed her, the mother rushed to me and quickly escorted me out of the door, stuttering apologies and asking forgiveness. I went with her and said that her daughter was probably not ready for me yet ... but that I would call back and see her. This I did the very next morning. The Sacred Heart picture was back in its place (without the glass) and this time it was the daughter who apologised effusively. I told her that anger was as natural an emotion as sadness at a death and that she would probably feel all the more healthy for being able to express it. 'But will God forgive me, Father?' was her plaintive question. 'Didn't God give you the gift of anger as well as tears?' I said.

As well as saying prayers with the family on such an occasion, a priest may be able to give a lot of consolation by simply holding hands and giving warm and gentle embraces.

The funeral homily is something that a priest will have to struggle with continually. And I believe that it is more important to be sincere than to be original ... and above all to be accurate. If the priest decides to offer sympathy to the family, he must not forget to mention them all. It has happened, it is happening, and probably will continue to happen that a priest may offer his sympathy to the children and forget to mention the spouse. It may sound silly, it is silly, but it does happen ... not intentionally, I might add, but certainly carelessly. And yet even this points to the simple fact that the priest is human and so will make mistakes. It is a shame that a priest may be severely criticised for making a mistake, even though it is one that he 'should' not make.

Because of the fact that I can no longer serve as a parish curate, I find myself growing in admiration for my fellow priests. It must be said that they are generally a group of fairly dedicated men who serve their people generously and with great commitment. People sometimes tend to put a priest down if he makes mistakes; and maybe the priest may be one of those who fumble and futter their way through jobs because that is their nature. I am not trying to excuse the lazy man who puts his own needs and likes before those of his people: the man who closes up the parochial house at 7 p.m. and retires to his room to watch his favourite television programmes; or the man who arranges the time of Masses to suit his golfing days (I use the word 'days' deliberately in this context).

It is very important that a priest have a few hobbies to give a bit of balance to his life. Golf is one of those activities which a number of priests enjoy and it is a healthy pastime. I was never adept at any outdoor sport and I imagine that even if I were healthy and played a game of golf, I'd probably have a handicap of thirty! I used to enjoy a game of snooker but even that is too much for me now, so I content myself with reading, writing and a good film on television. Just now, I am preoccupied with learning to drive a hand-controlled car. The technique is different but I have come to appreciate the Irish Wheelchair Association which has provided me with an excellent driving instructor. I find that I am so involved with learning the practical adjustments that I have not been able to allow myself to sit with the emotional aspects of having to adjust to this new way of being. While my legs are getting more and more out of control, I think it is important that I exercise control over my life itself. It is also another challenge which I am taking on and hopefully if I master the controls and get through the driving-test it will become another hill which I will have climbed myself. I believe that every disabled person wants to remain as independent as possible. The obligation may rest on the disabled person to make his/her needs known and then those with responsibility and authority should respond with everything at their disposal to facilitate the person. I am now very conscious of churches and public buildings which do not have ramps which would enable a person in a wheelchair to enter on his/her own volition. I may have to start a campaign to have ramps available in sanctuaries!

Who supports the Priest?

People often talk about the loneliness of the priest's life. Being without a wife and children, there is the danger of the celibate man shunning all relationships and running away from all forms of intimacy and closeness. This is a difficulty that every priest must face so as not to become totally trapped within the 'clerical niche'. And it might surprise some people to hear me say that good relationships with fellow-priests are a *sine qua non* of the priesthood. If a priest is not able to relate humanly and fully with at least some of his colleagues then his sense of loneliness will be heightened considerably.

I have already spoken of the priests' fraternity to which I belong. But as well as that I am blessed with a few special friends in priesthood, both within the diocese itself and among my own classmates. I'm not sure if I could have survived without them. I pray with them, socialise with them and go on holidays with them. And I openly admit to loving them. That may not be easy for some people to hear but then people's knowledge and experience of love usually involves physical and genital expression.Within the married state that is the most intimate and personal expression of love between a man and a woman. Yet fathers love their children; mothers love their children and such love is strong and real and motivates parents to give of themselves for their children. It is not unknown for a parent to rush into a blazing house to try to save his/her children if they happen to be trapped within. This is a very special type of love. I believe that I would go to any lengths to give support and counsel to my own priest-friends. Indeed, since I became ill, I have found great comfort and support from my priest-friends. Their visits and telephone calls are deeply appreciated. Just recently I was hoping to visit the Continent on holiday with my two closest friends. We had talked about the trip and began to look at dates and times. Unfortunately, my body had weakened

considerably during these past few months and my two friends
came to ask me what sort of holiday would suit me. I stated simply
that I would not be able to travel abroad and would probably stay
in Ireland. They immediately said that they would do the same so
that we could share time together. And they did this without leaving me to carry any guilt.

A number of years ago one of these friends, Fr Colm O' Doherty
was conducting a youth retreat with me. We were giving it to a
mixed group of teenagers. The theme of the retreat was 'love' and
we hoped to try to help them to try to grapple with the notion of
unconditional love ... Matthew 5 was to be the holding Scripture
text. During the day, the teenagers kept bringing up the idea of
sexual, genital love which is fairly natural for growing teenagers
to discuss. It was not easy for them to understand the way God
loves us. Even the most perfect loving relationship is but a poor reflection of the way God loves us. Anyway, we struggled through
the day with them and at least they stayed with us ... or so we
thought. The close of the day was to be the celebration of the
Eucharist. For this we gathered round in a circle with Colm and
myself sitting opposite each other in the circle. We had decided on
a dialogue homily between Colm and myself leaving space for
any of the young people to enter with their thoughts. They were
very quiet as Colm began the homily. I took up a few points to try
to widen the searching but there was still no response. Then Colm
said quite naturally, 'Do you see that man over there?' (pointing to
me) 'Well, I love him.' And immediately there was a response.
Words like 'homo', 'pouf', 'queer boy' immediately were thrown
out mixed in with giggles and laughter. The homily really opened
up then as we challenged them on their assumptions and prejudices. When Jesus washed the feet of his apostles, was he not loving
them? When Jesus allowed Mary to wash his feet with her tears
and wipe them away with her hair, was he not loving her? Are we
not degrading the marriage act by presuming it is a normal way of
loving between two single people? But the young people of today
are as much a product of their parents as they are of the society in
which they live. While parents may give a very traditionalist view
of sex and love which may be straight-laced and conservative,

society may give the impression that sexual love is a normal way for two young people to be close. Striking a correct and healthy balance takes a lot of growing up, developing and maturing.

That a priest could and might have a relationship with a woman is a subject that at least is being looked at and discussed today. There is even a bigger problem here in seeing this type of loving within the celibate context. Celibacy is part and parcel of the priesthood which I have accepted but that does not mean that I won't have 'bad thoughts'. I can appreciate a beautiful woman as much as anyone. Several years ago I was asked to speak to a group of young men who were considering entering a seminary to train for the priesthood. I was assisting another priest who was the main speaker. Part of the day was an open forum session. One of the questions that was thrown at us was, 'Do you ever feel attracted to a nice-looking woman?' I foolishly jumped in to try to answer the question. I admitted to being able to recognise a beautiful woman if I saw one and said that it was nice for the 'ego' if she responded even with a pleasant smile. But I went on and said that at times in a busy urbanised parochial house, a priest may have a lot of callers. On one particular night after evening Mass, I returned to the parochial house to find a line of about twenty people waiting to see the priest. I began to deal with their requests as best I could. None of them was too serious – Mass cards, baptismal forms, passport forms – and I was getting through them as well as I could. Then there entered a beautiful young girl with a smile all over her face and she was looking for a reference for a job … possibly the reason for the lovely smile. She was an intelligent young woman as well and we became involved in pleasant conversation. She was easy to talk to and pleasant to look at … but then I was cut off by the senior priest who said that that was probably not the way to deal with such a situation. 'You should not give extra time to a woman because her looks please you,' he said with great authority and warned me that I might have been 'flirting' with the lady. Maybe I was, but not consciously; I was simply enjoying her company. Every man likes to be noticed by a fine-looking young woman but that does not mean that he wants to become involved with her. Liking a young woman, even loving her, is very different from falling in love with her. But it is obvious that priests do fall in love with women. It is, of course, a fact that priests leave the priesthood and marry. This could only have happened if the priest falls in love with a woman. People are very quick to condemn in such a situation and their condemnation is more than often directed against the woman than the priest. I do not wish to get involved in that argument as I believe it to be a foolish one. If two adults decide to marry then it must be a mutual decision. What people may not give thought to is the serious soul-searching that both the priest and the woman go through. It is never a decision taken lightly. And I know of several priests who would love to remain on as priests after marriage. But the rule is strict and as yet no exceptions have been made. People argue that married people cannot 'walk away' from their vows, and they fail to understand that celibacy is a Church law and, even though married, the priest is still a priest but he cannot exercise his priestly functions. And there are priests who, although they may have fallen in love with a woman decide to remain on in the priesthood and leave the woman. These are very hidden wounds which a priest has to carry alone, but if he makes such a decision he finds his happiness in continuing to be a priest. And again it is a mutually agreed decision and the woman is prepared to let him go and carry on his mission. This must be a very distressing time for both priest and woman.

But there is the situation whereby the priest finds a woman with whom he relates as a close friend. She may be married or single but she is one who listens as only a woman can, offers friendship without compromising either herself or the priest and even helps the priest to discover qualities of character within himself which he may have been afraid to look at or admit. A priest said recently that there was the myth of the old priest who had the reputation of being 'a holy man', growing old with one hand on the rosary beads and the other on a bottle of whiskey; whereas the younger priest today can safely put both his arms around a woman and then leave to go to prayer.

It is only in recent times that Irishmen have comfortably expressed their feelings. Today they will tell their children of their love for them and openly show signs of affection in the home.

Thankfully priests are more prepared to show signs of affection to men, women and children. When I was in parish, I used make a point each Christmas and Easter night of processing down the aisle to greet the people as they left the Church. I shook as many men's hands as I could and embraced and kissed the women and children. I would find myself going back to the sacristy covered in all sorts of lipstick. When I was in Creggan parish, I was able to stand in the ambo and tell my people that I loved them. I meant it because it was true. I regretted not having the courage to do the same in my first parish. But I was only growing up then and was a bit afraid of what I was feeling. I would like to think that priests do love their people. I'm sure some priests must be thinking I am a bit crazed ... but of this I am sure: if a priest spends himself for his people over a number of years, they begin to love him. Maybe priests have a problem with the word 'love'... and that would be even sadder.

If a priest trusts his gut and is not afraid of himself, he will find great help from the love of a woman. Surely a priest's life must know of human happiness, and being able to relate in a human fashion is as much the right of the celibate as the married person. This is friendship, intimacy, and love and it does not involve genital intimacy. Some people may say the risk is too great and that may be true for some priests and some women, but it cannot be accepted as a general rule. I can say that there are a few women in my life – both married and single – and I am proud to be able to have them as my friends. They have helped me to understand more about myself than I could have learned from a book; and they have not been afraid to tell me the truth. As a young priest I worked hard and it was as woman who told me that I was becoming a workaholic. I loved and still love saying Mass and it was a woman who said to me that it did not show on my face (and I'm still working on that one). I used to wear clothes until they wore out and it was a woman who drew my attention to my dress.

It may be important to say that not all priests are living from day to day trying to choose between their priesthood and a woman. The priests whom I know are generally very happy men who have learned to cope with life's difficulties. They do not go around under a cloud worrying and struggling with their vocation. Many of them worry about more foolish things, like the financial statement of the parish or what will they buy their housekeepers for Christmas.

I believe it to be a much sadder state of affairs when a priest begins to take refuge in a bottle. And it is to the credit of the Irish people that they are so sympathetic to the alcoholic priest. It is not unknown for parishioners to take their priest home if they find him in an unfit state in some hotel. There is something attractive about a priest whose weaknesses are open to view. The priest who drinks alone and at home is often in a much sadder situation. He may not be able to do anything about his loneliness and he hides away from all company, even his own fellow-priests. I am not saying that having a personal relationship with a woman will automatically prevent a priest from becoming an alcoholic person. There are many married couples who could testify to the opposite, but priests may be more susceptible to seeking refuge in a bottle or something else to escape from personal loneliness. If a priest is not able to form good relationships with his priests or his parishioners, then a woman friend is not going to be his solution. Celibacy is not about locking oneself away from human contact; in fact it is more about being able to relate with men and women in a human and wholesome way. Celibacy is not the denial of the human needs in the priest; it is a call to reach out to others and even *an other* and to love. This of itself means being vulnerable, being trusting and risking. It involves friendship which is intimate and caring and which takes account of the boundaries necessary in any relationship. Priests are in the business of loving – 'A new commandment I give you, love one another.' Can we priests stand at an altar and tell people of God's love for them without our willingness to love them? It is too easy to speak of loving all my people without my loving individuals as individuals.

I am not denying the pain of celibacy nor would I want to make it out as life-time imprisonment of solitary confinement. Even married couples can find themselves alone at the very depths of their beings. And if a married man or woman is living out his/her relationship according to accepted 'catholic' standards, then he/she is a celibate to all other people ... yet that need not prevent them from having close friendships with other individuals. Celibacy is a call to love in a very special way. It acknowledges human attraction, making space for another in one's life and even being affectionate.

I personally regretted failing to show real affection to my father while he lived. As the undertaker closed the lid on his coffin, I swore to myself that I would not make the same mistake with my mother and brothers and sisters. There was no doubt in my mind that my father loved me and I loved him. I still remember the strength of his hand as he used to walk with me and my younger brother every Sunday afternoon. And I can remember the words of my mother after his death, 'He was so proud of you, that in spite of all the financial worries, you made it to the priesthood.' How I would have loved to have heard him saying those words to me. But I did not know how I was going to carry out my wish. It happened without planning. I was saying an anniversary Mass for my father the following year. The family was all gathered, including little nieces and nephews. Everything went as normal until it came to the sign of peace. I paused and looked at my family and as I was beginning to say a few words on this, I found tears rolling down my face and I just could not stop them. I heard one of my nieces saying, 'Look, uncle Jimmy is crying.' I then proceeded to greet each and every one of them to tell them of my love. After that I could not wait to finish the Mass as quickly as possible. I then disappeared up to one of the bedrooms and sat on the edge of the bed feeling highly embarrassed. After a few minutes, two of my sisters came to the door and asked was I coming down for a cup of tea. I said that I felt rotten by making such a fool of myself. But one of my sisters said, 'That was the nicest gift you ever gave to us, Jimmy. Now, come on down and have the tea.' I believe something special happened to my family that night. The tea was good, the crack was great and I felt as light as a feather driving back to the parochial house that night. Something also had happened to me. Something was released within me and I found myself gain-ing in confidence with people. I began to trust my gut reaction with people and if embraces, hugs and kisses seemed appropriate, I gave them freely and unashamedly. And it must be said that people responded with a greater freedom than I could ever have imagined. It was I who had the hangups, not them.

I believe that a priest can have a real and healthy relationship with a woman. He may have to be careful not to give scandal to the 'weaker brethren' but it does not mean that he hide himself away with his woman friend. I believe each can take care of the other and trust themselves to each other in a open and caring fashion. I remember with some humour an older priest speaking to me and Colm O'Doherty and Brian Brady. We were ranging over many subjects that night and when we came to discuss the notion of celibacy, the old priest got up from his chair and said the Church is a bit like a football team. 'Did you ever see,' he said, 'a line of defenders lining up in front of a free kick? They stand there with there hands crossed over their front to protect a very vulnerable are?' As he spoke, he began hopping about his sitting room with his hands crossed in front of him. 'That's the Church! Protect, protect, protect!' he said, as we fell over in laughter.

I do not intend here to exhaust what could be said on the subject of celibacy. You will be able to find better and more theological works on the subject; I'm more interested in trying to speak about attitudes and unhealthy prejudices. Of course it is a struggle; so too is marriage; so too is the single life. To expect that it would be otherwise would be rather foolish. The priest like every other human is a sexual person and he has to learn to integrate his sexuality into his life and love. Loving itself is difficult, as are relationships, but the answer will not be found in running away from them. And I believe the answer is found in the ordinary everyday relationships which fill a priest's life. Sometimes a film like 'The Thornbirds' can give a rather distorted notion of a priest's womanly relationships ... or the novel which fantasises about a priest having full sexual intercourse with a woman and then struggling to live a 'double life'. This is not the struggle of the celibate priest ... his struggle will lie in loving a woman without expressing it genitally and then trying to integrate such loving into his life without compromising either the woman or himself. Nor is it a question of a balancing act where both the priest and the woman try to walk a narrow line down a narrow road strewn with broken glass and hidden mines ready to explode at the slightest touch.

A priest can love and remain a priest or else we are in the wrong world. And I am not advocating that every priest must go out and find a woman friend. But if he has got one, then love her dearly and truly and thank God for the gift of such a woman. It is an important facet of being human to be able to receive as well as give love. In fact if we think of love as only giving then we may have to re-learn its true meaning. While Jesus Christ gave his very life as an expression of his great love for all of us, he was also known as a person who could receive love ... and not just from his apostles, but from individuals like Magdalene, Mary, Martha and Lazarus over whose tomb he wept. He was open to receiving love from these friends and it was well-known and acknowledged.

Before I leave this subject I think it must be said that priests can survive and survive quite well without venturing into a personal relationship with a woman. I would not like to think that I am giving the impression that unless a priest has a special woman friend, that he is lacking in something. In the normal routine of parish work, a priest will come up against many women with whom he will establish healthy and heart-warming friendships. I oftentimes thank God for my sisters and nieces, but they too are special women in my life.

Maybe we priests could challenge a modern misconception of love which seems to define it within erotic terms ... because 'falling in love' is a sex-linked erotic experience (and basically a very immature way of relating). Stable, healthy marriages witness to the permanence and indissolubility of marriage, and they challenge the idea of marriages as being temporary and unfaithful as portrayed in the modern novel, film or television 'soap'. Could not priests witness to the goodness of love in human relationships which is not dependent upon erotic sexual expression? Is this not what the Church means when it talks of celibacy as being eschatalogical – that it points forward to a newer and better world 'where there is neither marriage nor giving in marriage'?

His relationship with women will be one of the major challenges to the priest's own self – will he remain 'safe and snug' within the 'collared institution' or will he be big enough to step outside and risk living as a human person? Clerical dress is changing before our very eyes and although there have been a few warnings issued from episcopal circles it has been so quickly accepted by people that the warnings became to sound foolish.

I think it would be wrong to see this change as something dramatic, but it is not unusual to see a priest wearing coloured jumpers and grey slacks. It may be an unconscious way for the priest to move slightly away from his 'clerical niche'. Nor is it a way for the priest to try to disguise himself. Within six months in a parish, a priest is usually known by the majority of his parishioners. I personally find it more relaxing to be able to throw on a brightly coloured jumper and even in the summer to lay aside the clerical collar itself. There may be times when this is inappropriate, but I trust the good sense of the priest to recognise these times. If I were going to say a public Mass or to attend a wake-house, I would always try to dress properly. In recent months I wrote a song to which a friend of mine put the music, and there were four priests singing the harmonies and the chorus. We were asked to appear on Sir Harry Secombe's 'Highway Show'. While we appeared in the film as priests dressed in formal black suits and white collars, the producer asked us to dress a bit more casually when we were singing the song. For us that meant fairly dark trousers, open-necked shirts and coloured jumpers. When I watched the film eventually on television, I had to laugh at how we looked. A lady summed it up perfectly when she said that we seemed to be advertising for some men's wear shop. I had to admit it looked a bit silly although the producer was pleased enough with our appearance. When I go on holiday with my priest-friends, we lay aside the black altogether. It helps us to be private and inconspicuous.

I once holidayed with seven of my own classmates and we booked a large caravan in a holiday resort. We had a couple of cars between us so that we could follow our own pursuits. The only time that we were together was at night when we returned to the caravan. Then we shared experiences, laughed a little or even played a few hands of poker. We were in the middle of a game one night when a knock came to the door. Upon opening it, we discovered that it was the gentleman from the neighbouring caravan. He asked to be excused and wondered would we like to share some of his home-made soup. He was carrying a large pot with steam issuing from it. We welcomed him in and thanked him. Then he said, 'I presume you are priests.' Naturally we enquired as to how he was able to recognise us. He said, 'I see you go to the Church each day and I notice there are never any females with you.' He actually happened to be a French chef. We laughed at his powers of observation and afterwards wondered what he would have thought of us if any females had visited us.

I'm not sure why priests feel obliged to wear their clerical dress when on holiday ... especially when they go to the Continent. There are times and places when it would be normal, as, for example, when a priest may be going to Lourdes with his parishioners.

I have been to Lourdes several times but shortly after I had been diagnosed as having Multiple Sclerosis, I decided to go to Lourdes accompanied by my friend, Colm O' Doherty. We went as 'private pilgrims' and decided not to wear the clerical dress. We did this because we wanted to make a quiet pilgrimage and avoid being hassled in any way by other pilgrims. We were in an hotel with a group of pilgrims from the South of Ireland. They were being shepherded by their own priest and the people at whose table we sat began to wonder about us. We had obvious Irish accents but we did not join the other pilgrims on their various exercises. The simple reason for that was that I just was not well enough, but Colm and I got through the exercises at our own pace. Towards the end of the week the table-guests began to pick up some courage to ask us a few questions. Were we journalists writing up a story? Were we Protestants making investigations about Marian devotion? Were we atheists seeking answers to questions? We played the game along with them and it became very much part of the meal-chat. The official priest of the party gave us a very wide berth because I believe he did not wish to interfere in our business which was really rather courteous of him. But on the final day, he joined the table and we entered into conversation with him. Finally he asked without any hesitation, 'Excuse me fellows, but do you mind me asking you, "are you priests?"' 'Yes,' we said, 'we are.' The rest of the people laughed and then expressed a little annoyance, 'Why didn't you tell us you were priests?'

'Because,' we said, 'you never asked us!'

Money

A great bone of contention that exists between priests and people is the question of money. 'Those priests are always looking for money,' is a common phrase on many people's lips. Yet in fact I know that priests find it a very difficult subject about which to speak. Priests are responsible for the financial running of a parish and they have to try to ensure that the parish plant survives. They have to deal with the usual problems that face most business people, and yet they would have very little training in such matters. Because of my own family background, I literally never saw a cheque-book until I became a priest. If a priest is in a parish, he has to pay the typical bills that are part and parcel of maintaining buildings – heating, electricity and wages. The priest in the Derry Diocese now gets a basic wage and out of that he must pay for his car, his food, his holidays, his clothes and the furniture for his house. I believe it would be true to say that most priests can survive quite comfortably on what he receives ... but it would be also true to say that when a priest asks for money from the altar it would be going towards the maintenance of the parish buildings, and certainly not for himself.

I remember a young man who was always saying to me that I was in a 'cushy number'. He kept gibing me so often that I eventually put him to a test. 'Would you be willing to swop your wage-packet for mine next month?' I asked him. 'I'll put my cheque in an envelope and I will swop it directly with your monthly cheque.' 'No problem,' he said. When the end of the month came round we met in order to make the exchange. 'What do you get?' he asked. 'Well, according to you,' I said, 'it's plenty and furthermore I do not have an idea of what you get but I am willing to gamble that if we make the swop, I'll come off better.' He hesitated, squared himself up but backed away laughing, 'You are trying to pull a fast one one me.' I stood holding out my envelope but he baulked at the offer. He never mentioned money after that.

It might be worth mentioning here that priests do not take a vow of poverty but I believe it would be appropriate that they do not have a high life-style. Not many priests can actually afford a high life-style anyway, although some may have wealthy families that are generous to them. It is their business what they do with their money. It might also surprise some people to know that there are priests who are often in debt. My major expenditure would be buying and maintaining a car. In fact for the first number of years in priesthood, I received help from my family to buy clothes. People in parishes are very generous to a priest. At Christmastime I would usually get enough new jumpers, shirts, socks, handkerchiefs to do me for most of the coming year. I was in the priesthood a number of years before I could afford a continental holiday. There is one thing that I would say for certain, men do not join the priesthood for the money! If that happened to be the big attraction, there would not be such a shortage of priests! And there is no such thing as overtime, double-time or bonuses. In the past twenty years the culture of the country has changed so much that most working families possess a motor-car. There are few homes that do not have a television set and video. These are not justifying reasons for the priest to possess all the possible luxuries, but I see no reason why he should not possess them if he so wishes. Again the first video which I ever had was presented to me by an organisation which I had served for some years and then had to leave because of my sickness ... and I enjoy having it. When a group of priests was recently discussing their financial situations, one particular priest admitted to giving away about £1,000 per year in handouts ... and that is not unusual in an urbanised setting where living standards are poor. And when people come to a parochial house looking for money, the priest does try to assess their needs and give accordingly. Everybody promises to repay the money but in the twenty-four years that I have been priesting, only two people ever returned to offer repayment. I believe that most priests realise that such monies will not be returned and they do not begrudge it. But, like anybody, they do not like being 'conned'. Sometimes we can admire the stories which are created in order to get money from us.

I remember being in the parochial house one day and the parish priest told me of a young lad who had come to the door seeking money. 'He was a student,' said the parish priest, 'and he needed a few pounds which I gave him.' About an hour later a lady came to the door to see me. 'I may be completely wrong, Father, but there is this young lad down in my mother's house and he has gathered in several families telling them that he is a clerical student and he is on a special mission. I feel uneasy about him and I wonder if you would come to meet him.' I immediately took the lady in my car and drove to the house. There were about a dozen people in the sitting-room listening to this young man. He gave me a great welcome and proceeded with his story. He claimed that he belonged to a particular order and that part of his training was to wander the country for six months learning to survive. He spoke with a strong Dublin accent and he used the names of priests in the Derry Diocese whom he knew. He was quite remarkable both in the flow of his words and the content of his stories. But I too felt very uneasy. Then one of the visitors asked him about his vocation. 'When did you realise you had a vocation?' His answer convinced me that something was badly wrong. 'Well,' he said, 'it was like a flashing light across the sky and the voice of God was in it.' I immediately said, 'That's enough, young lad, I think we should have a talk in private.' The people left the room and the confrontation began. He did not like my tone and in fact tried to turn the tables on me. 'If you touch me,' he said, 'I'll have the police here in five minutes.' I went and called one of the men to join us in the room and told him that I wanted him to witness what was going on. But the young man said, 'Take me to your parish priest. I have already met him and he is a gentleman.' I then realised that this was the young man who had been cordially received by the parish priest. But I took him with me back to the parochial house. The parish priest was beginning to offer us a great welcome when I told him that I thought that the young man was a fraud … but he was quite brazen and accused me of harrassing him. We questioned him for some time and finally I said that I would prefer to call in the police. 'Go ahead,' said the student. The parish priest was still advising caution. But I went to the telephone and had actually dialed two numbers when the student spoke, this time using a strong Derry accent. He told us his real name and the parish in which he lived. I rang the priests there to see if they knew him. They knew everything about him and apparently he had quite a record of doing the same prank in various places. His policy would have been to go to a family, gain their confidence, receive presents of money and usually manage to stay the night in the house ... except that he rose in the middle of the night, stole whatever valuables were in sight and disappear. The priests from the other parish agreed to collect him and return him to his home.

Yet it would be fairly customary now that priests would put in the parish bulletin the annual financial statement so that people would be able to see for themselves the income of the parish and the various items of expenditure. I believe this to be a very useful exercise and it helps to quieten sarcastic remarks about the priest and money. And I have found from my own personal experience that if a priest tells his people exactly why he may need extra money in the weekly collection, then they respond with tremendous generosity. During my short time as Administrator in St Mary's Parish, Creggan, I decided, with the support of the other priests and the full backing of the Parish Council, to do a major renovation job in the parish church. As it is a mensal parish, I also needed the permission of the bishop. He gave the plans his total support. But I thought it would be a wise thing if we tried to involve the people as closely as possible. My architect created a model of the work which I had displayed in the Church and before work began I held public meetings in the Church each week and sought suggestions and comments. One of the most practical ideas that came from those meetings was a request for a large ramp to be built at the side door for prams and wheelchairs. When full consultation had taken place and the people had received as much information about the proposed work, all the priests of the parish spoke on one particular Sunday about the money that would be needed and what we would be asking from the people. But even then I found that piece of work very difficult. I was conscious of the fact that many of the Creggan people were unem-

ployed, families were large and money was scarce. Yet they responded beyond my wildest expectations ... the weekly collection almost doubled immediately and people were calling to the
parochial house with private donations, probably some of their
meagre savings, but typically generous. I used to express my
thanks in the parish bulletin for such gifts and I can still remember
a group of elderly people calling to see me with money which they
had collected and they explicitly asked me not to write it up in the
bulletin and simply to say it was an anonymous gift ... not only
generous but modest. While there are people who never think of
giving any money to the upkeep of their local churches, the generosity of people cannot be underestimated. And when people see
the money being put to good use, they give willingly.

Authority

I heard an American priest use the phrase, 'no fuss, no rust, no lust'. It was his colloquial way of speaking about obedience, poverty, and chastity. The priest, on his ordination day, promises obedience to his bishop and his successors. There is a special relationship that exists between a priest and his bishop. Central to it would be the notion of authority and obedience. I had the very special role of being diocesan secretary to my bishop for two years. I personally was not keen on the nature of the job itself as I preferred to work directly with people themselves; yet it opened my eyes to the role of a bishop and his work. Bishop Daly, even when a curate, was a busy dedicated man; his busy-ness and dedication were carried over into his new position within the Church. I came to admire not only his work-rate but also his organising ability.

One of the most difficult tasks of a bishop is the transferral of priests from one parish to another. And it is then a priest obeys without question ... although I must say that there can be consultation to some degree. Even as I write, the bishop has asked the priests' council to investigate the whole system of 'changes' and prepare some way that would be mutually agreeable to both bishop and priests (without taking away the bishop's sight to transfer a person if the need so requires). But the authority that impinges more on a priest's life is the authority exercised over him by his parish priest. Again the problem can go back to the whole idea of team-ministry.

I believe that the Second Vatican Council has opened up new models of Church which as yet have not filtered down to the ground level. The hierarchial structure and model has been one out of which we have lived and worked for many years ... and this model favoured the idea of authority issuing from the 'top' downwards, and it was unquestioned. The idea of Church as being *The*

People of God has not yet been translated into everyday living terms. The notion of the Church as being prophetic is seen to apply to other countries and not Ireland. We have grown up with priests in parishes providing essential services like the sacraments or working as teachers in schools and it is almost impossible for us to think that priests might work out of a different pastoral setting. Again the idea that basic Christian communities are for other countries and not our own is accepted without question. And I am not making a plea here for priests to go U.D.I. I believe in the need for some rational way of discovering the needs of the people and then trying to respond to those needs. I would be a bit wary of priests moving into the political scene. Priests must be involved in politics insofar as they are living and working with people in real life ... but party politics is a different ball-game and by the very fact that we are ordained ministers of the Church, we are involved with a kingdom 'not of this world'. That does not prevent us from being able to challenge the state and its government if it is failing to give to people their proper rights. If, as a result of civil government, the poor are getting poorer and the rich getting richer, then it is up to the Church to inform itself why this is so and to speak out loudly and clearly. In recent years the Church has stated its support for the poor, but this may need more definite action from the Church if its words are to prove authentic.

At times it can be embarrassing for the Church if a priest seems to stand outside its local structures and plough his own furrow, especially if this is marked by bitter remarks and sardonic accusations. Healthy debate is one thing but bitterness and rancour is another. It can be hard enough being a priest at times because of the loneliness and sense of isolation one may experience because of one's position; it must be ten times more lonely for a priest who steps outside his normal support system. There are no such things as trade unions for priests and I do not think that I would favour them; but there is a system even within our Church for conciliation between priest and bishop if that were needed.

I'm wondering even as I write whether people are a bit surprised or even shocked at the fact that priests may not be able to agree on certain policy matters or even simple ways of approaching problems. But I must re-emphasise again that we are only human. It is a common thing for a modern-day business to have personnel managers who would be able to respond to the particular needs of a worker and help him/her dovetail into the entire work-force. And while it is true to say that there can be disagreements between priests, I believe it to be to the credit of priests that they do not wash their dirty linen in public... and possibly it is even more to their credit that they can discover a way of working together that does not bring discredit on anybody.

I suppose priests are in a rare situation. They are in a position where their socialising is done with their fellow-workers, and if there is tension in the work situation, it can spill over into their everyday living. This can be very difficult if they happen to be living in the same house. But if they can learn to cope with this and try to talk through their problems then they will become the better men because of that and, hopefully, the better priests. The 'authority syndrome' can aggravate the situation if the one in charge and with the authority uses his position to negate all communication and thereby refuses to listen to another man's viewpoint. In reality this is an abuse of authority and maybe it is more true to say that some priests do not know how to exercise authority. The people can feel this as well when a priest begins to make his own little rules for a parish and then imposes them on his people. While this may be hurtful for the people, it is a very sad situation and there may be no real resolution to it. But people are often wiser than priests sometimes think and they are able to get on with their lives in spite of silly regulations formulated by the priest. But, truth to say, people can sometimes demand more than the priest can give. I remember being awakened from my sleep one night at about 3 a.m. It always takes a few seconds before one can easily register and be in touch with reality at that time in the morning. 'Could you come and pick me up, Father?' I heard a voice ask. 'Pardon?' I said, 'What's the problem?' It was the voice of a young man but there were a few other voices in the background. 'Well, you see, it's like this, Father, we were out at a bit of a party tonight and we stayed a bit late and all the taxis have stopped working

and I was wondering if you would give us a life home.' I still do not
know whether it was shock, anger or total disbelief that made me
refuse; nor was I sure if I were not in some dream. Thankfully such
requests are rare but that they happen at all makes me wonder a
little about how some people may see the priest ... a man for all
seasons and all events and all possible eventualities.

And it is true that as a man matures in his work as a priest, he
learns to discern the urgent, the emergency, the real and to respond in ways that are practical and useful. The 'sacristy priest',
while still alive in places, is gradually becoming a dying breed.
Priests find themselves becoming involved in people's lives in
many different ways – and not merely as the man who brings and
distributes the sacraments – but hopefully as the man who is
interested in spreading the kingdom of God and its values; and
this cannot be limited to a Sunday morning or a First Friday. Nor
can it be contained within the walls of the local church building.

The Autumn

It was Keats who wrote the beautiful lines:
Season of mist and mellow fruitfulness,
Close bosom friend of the maturing sun.

These lines seem to give the impression that coming to fruition is a gentle process, and maybe that is true of nature. The flora may come to maturation spontaneously and without any obvious difficulties. But being human seems to involve a little more effort. People talk of the forties as being a more difficult stage in the development of the human person. Maybe it is part of the seven-year process and humans have to deal with new inner feelings. For the ordinary man or woman, it is often the stage when their growing children begin to leave the home and to establish homes of their own. Women talk of the menopausal stage that may begin to take place at this time of life ... and it is said that men have a corresponding stage in their own lives. It can also be a time in a man's life when he is coming to the fulness of his career. He may have climbed the ladder of success and promotion within his particular firm and there may be little else to achieve there. So it can become a time of ensuring his comfort and making the necessary arrangements for future retirement. The need for security becomes very important and people will try to ensure that their future years are well provided for.

Yet the priest may find himself in a very different situation. He has reached his forties and he is still a curate and may remain so until his fifties. The situation in our diocese is such that a priest at forty knows that the prospect of him becoming a parish priest is still far away. This is simply part of the system in which we find ourselves. Becoming a parish priest follows in seniority and one knows just how many priests are ahead of one. There are several difficulties in such a system. If a man has been priesting for over twenty years in various parishes, doing the same types of jobs each day of each week of each year, he may find himself slipping into a type of rut. There are no new surprises, no sense of excitement, no goals to reach for and he can become content with simply filling in his time ... doing his duties, fulfilling his obligations but with little spark or enthusiasm. His daily routine becomes a job to do and he does it without much thinking. It can be a difficult time especially if a priest allows this to become mundane. If a priest is caught in this mind-set, then anything that disturbs his daily routine becomes an act of interference. He has little responsibility in the true sense of that word and he may begin to wilt.

A further danger is that he may begin to wait, passively, for his appointment as a parish priest and by the time that comes, he accepts the post and 'retires' gracefully. He may hope to be appointed to a parish which has one or two curates whom he hopes will do all the peripheral jobs – the youth club, the bingo session, the parochial dances, the bowls club, the football club – and allow him to do the 'big' work, like administration of the schools. By the time he becomes parish priest, all the life in him has been stubbed out and he wants as little bother as possible. I believe this to be a very human thing and I do not want to take away from the parish priests who tackle their new responsibility with verve and renewed energy.

The whole scene can take on a funny quirk when a parish priest is 'landed' with an over-enthusiastic curate who wants change and renewal and begins coming to the parish priest with all sorts of new ideas, which may mean that the parish priest has to become involved if they are to work successfully. Or contrariwise, the parish priest may enter a parish with many new ideas himself which he had always wanted to try and finds that his curate could not be bothered. The curate may prefer his room and his books and is quite content with the minimum. He may not want to hear of parish renewal or charismatic movements. It is very difficult to enthuse another person with your ideas if he sees either little point in them or is afraid of the extra work that may be involved.

Many years ago I used get very excited about youth retreats. It was a great challenge for the priest to try to meet with a group of young strangers and speak the Gospel message to them and, in the middle of it all, discover that very few of the young people actually had a living faith in either God himself or in the Church. Older priests would say to me, 'Why spend so much of your energy at that work, when that is the job of their parents?' Or another common remark would have been, 'You should not be working with young people in isolation from their parents or parish.' Yet there may have been something distinctly primitive or even missionary in such work which actually excited me. In time priests find the places where they would like to invest extra energy, whether it be the charismatic movement, the marriage encounter movement, the cursillo group, or youth groups. It is this diversity that helps to provide many extra services to a diocese and helps to meet the growing needs of our people today.

Perhaps a word of affirmation would not be out of place here. I have had to remove myself from the hurly-burly of parish life because of my sickness. Had I not developed Multiple Sclerosis, I would probably be in there struggling alongside of my fellow-priests. Now I am unable to do even the ordinary duties of a humble curate. I have not retired and the bishop has respected my wishes in this regard ... so I find myself working with varied little groupings – a youth group, a lay-fraternity group, a group of mothers and parents who are seeking some help with their own religious development, and being available to M.S. branches to offer help and guidance as well as being available to individuals coming to me for some advice and counselling ... so my days and weeks can still be fairly full. However I am able in some real sense to stand back from the parish set-up and observe my fellow-priests at work; and to be very honest, I am enthused at their work-rate, offering steady, consistent service. Each and every day of their lives is filled with appointments and duties which they carry out without complaint. They must be one of the few remaining work-forces who have never gone out on strike for better wages or improved conditions. And while the 'autumnal' priests may be waiting for their final appointments as parish priests, they remain at their posts giving persistent service.

People and priests talk sometimes about the 'characters' when they refer to parish priests who have built up reputations as men with rare and peculiar idiosyncracies. Every walk of life has them and priests are no exception. There is the story, which is probably fictional and yet carries a certain amount of truth, about the parish priest who continually preached about 'sin' each and every Sunday. The people became a bit frustrated about it and eventually wrote to the bishop about the matter. In a finely-worded letter the bishop asked the parish priest to preach about the Holy Spirit as it was coming near the Feast of Pentecost. What the parish priest did not know was that the bishop joined the congregation to listen to the sermon. After the Gospel had been read and the people sat back to listen, the parish priest began, 'Today I want to speak to you about the Holy Spirit and there is one thing that the Holy Spirit despises and that is *sin* ...' As I said, the story is more likely to be apocryphal but it does point to the rather strange habits which an older man my have grown accustomed to. And such stories remain alive because of the fact that the majority of priests maintain a good sense of the reality and consistently provide sterling service. In such context, the strange and bizarre are memorable and become part of the folk-lore and mythology that surrounds the lives of priests.

I can remember myself, when I was totally engrossed in the establishment of the Catholic Marriage Advisory Council, that many of my sermons at that time had marriage, the family, healthy relationships, continually recurring in my few words on a Sunday morning. I must have bored the minds and hearts of my congregations. I have already mentioned the wisdom of the older priests and the common sense which they have gathered over the years. I remember when working in Waterside parish as a young curate. It was a busy parish and even trying to keep the parish ticking over kept all the priests busy and active. At that time there was no full-time chaplain working in the hospital, so each of us took it in turn to cover the hospital calls on a rota basis. This meant that for one full week in each month, the priest on call had to be available to any and every emergency sick-call that came from any of the four hospitals and from the parish itself. It was not unusual to be called out at night and probably that could occur on two or three of the nights of one's week on call, and when it did one usually ended up feeling very exhausted and tired. I had just finished my week on call and I had been out on four separate nights. I went to bed on Saturday night relieved that my call duties were finished. I set my alarm for 8 o'clock in the morning so that I would be able to rise and say the 9 o'clock Mass in one of the out-churches. I jumped from my bed at 9.25 a.m. and immediately realised my mistake. I dressed as quickly as possible and went to see the parish priest because I had heard that if a priest failed to turn up for his Sunday Mass that he had to report it to the bishop. Rather sheepishly I went to the parish priest's door and knocked. I explained to him the predicament in which I had landed myself and wondered what to do. 'Sure, Jimmy,' said he, 'it could happen to a bishop. Now go and get some breakfast and you may expect a large crowd at the 11 0'clock Mass in the same little church, but I think the people will understand.' His easy way reassured me and when I went to say the 11 o'clock Mass there was not enough room in the church to hold all the people. My apology was readily accepted and when I said, 'If one of you sleeps in, you can always go to another Mass without anyone being any the wiser; but when a priest sleeps in, the whole parish knows,' the people expressed their appreciation by their laughter. And I remember telling myself that it would always be a good policy to be straight with my people and, if an apology was necessary, then it would be better to express it openly and cleanly.

But as the 'autumnal years' move along, priests may find themselves becoming involved in many different organisations. Their experience can be invaluable in several different fields. So as well as his normal parish work, a priest may find himself becoming attached to varied Commissions which have Diocesan significance – education, ecumenics, liturgy, emigration, priests' council, C.M.A.C., youth council and many more. Naturally these involve meetings which can really eat into a priest's time and energy. And even within the parish system itself, a priest may find himself caught by many meetings – the school boards, the parish council, the St Vincent de Paul, the Legion of Mary, the parochial hall committee and so on. Because of all these commitments, it is not unusual for a priest to find that he is beginning to suffer from 'burn-out'. This can lead to normal stress and strain and the only way to escape from it at times is to get out of the parish for a few days. I can remember at times in my earlier priesthood, that if I wanted to see a particular television programme, the only 'safe' place would be to go to my family home. Few men come to realise that they are suffering from possible 'burn-out' until natural age catches up with them. They suddenly find themselves attending their doctors for various ailments which are signs that the body is beginning to slow down. The afternoon nap becomes a part of the normal day. Alongside their aftershave and talc there begins to form a line of boxes of tablets needed to combat some peculiar symptoms. Some may even learn more about the meaning of depression and its awful effects. Perhaps I have had to cope with this earlier than usual because of my own disease. But most priests see aging as a relative thing. One does not really begin to age until one has spent a number of years as parish priest ... and even then it is the 'golden jubilee' that marks a man's age. So spending the 'autumnal years' as a curate may have the effect of rejuvenation. A priest can still say his daily Mass, attend his sick, do his baptisms, visit his homes and hear confessions. These duties in themselves are not beyond the capabilities of a man in his forties. And it can be easier for such a man to relate with a parish priest in his sixties.

I have heard priests speak of the terrible blackness which seems to descend on them at this stage ... a blackness marked by loneliness and lack of a sense of responsibility. I remember the frightening story of a priest who actually has reached his fifties and who still had to ask the parish priest for permission to write out a baptismal certificate. I could not fully appreciate this as it seemed so bizzare and especially against the background of my own diocese when many parochial houses had employed young secretaries to handle these and other matters.

There was a time when I would have been asked the question, 'Do you not regret not ever having married?' and subtly this question has become, 'Have you any regrets in becoming priest?' It's almost as if the questioner is saying, 'Well, you are too old now to get

married, so would you do it all over again?' I know that people do
not mean to be insulting, but I am also aware of the fact that life is
moving on and I am no longer the young priest. Actually I do not
carry regrets over the fact that I am not married and that is in no
way negating the things which I have said about the loneliness of
the priest. Of course, the house can be quiet at night and one does
not have the companionship of a wife with whom one can share
one's worries and troubles. And yet when one has lived as a celibate for over twenty years, one learns to accept that fact and actually one can jealously guard one's own private space. There is no
doubt that I miss having children of my own. I have always had a
fondness for children, extending from my own nieces and
nephews to children of the parish. Some people find children a bit
trying and yet I could spend hours chatting and playing with
them. I used babysit for my brother when I was a young teenager
and could gurgle with my young niece as she played in her carry-
cot. There was one day when I was watching her and getting the
table set for tea for my brother and his wife. My niece was cheer-
fully playing with her rattle. Just then a visitor came in looking for
my brother. It took less than two minutes to explain that he would
not be in from work for another twenty minutes. He thanked me
and left. I turned to the table to finish the preparations and quickly
noticed that my niece had gone very quiet. When I looked over at
her, she was lying back in her cot and her face was blue in colour.
I rushed over to her to see what had happened and I noticed that a
piece of plastic which must have been under the cot was torn. My
mind moved rapidly, 'She must have reached out of the cot and
tore a piece off and put it in her mouth.' I opened her mouth, put
my finger down her throat and caught hold of something which I
pulled... it was the plastic. I removed it completely and welcomed
her sudden cry and gasp for air. When my brother and his wife
returned, they found me gently nursing the child on my lap. I explained what had happened and they were grateful for the swift
action which I took. When I later told my mother what had happened, she quickly said, 'You should never take your eyes off a
child even for a moment.' She spoke from a lot of experience and I
tried to follow her advice in future. I presume many priests fanta-

sise about what children they might have had and we probably would not make any better parents than we are priests.

There are other dioceses where priests can expect to be appointed as parish priests in their forties. Some of my own classmates are already in that position and are now beginning their apprenticeship holding the reins. I believe it is a good age to accept responsibilities. A priest is young enough to innovate and experiment and wise enough not to do anything foolish.

I would like to offer a suggestion which might be picked up and kicked around a bit. The priests in our diocese are, at present, made parish priests in their mid or late fifties. They hold that position until their retirement at seventy-five. If it could be re-arranged that men would become parish priests between forty and forty-five and then retire from that position at sixty-five and take up a curacy again, it might help to alleviate some problems. It will probably create a new set of problems but maybe things would eventually balance themselves out. The biggest difficulty with such an arrangement would be that quite a number of priests would now have to agree to never becoming parish priests ... that they would willingly accept the fact that they were being passed over. I can immediately hear cries of disgust coming from priests even at making such a suggestion and even the accusation, 'That's alright for you, Jimmy, because you can never become a parish priest, but what about us who have been waiting for years for the opportunity of such a position?' I cannot disagree with that statement and I do realise that it would be a very big sacrifice. And yet there are men at this moment in our diocese who have 'retired' early from their positions as parish priests and have become curates again. And it is probably easier to settle in as a curate again at sixty-five instead of seventy-five. I am certainly not putting out my suggestions as the only possible solution, but by putting it out I may help to provoke some discussion about the problem and possibly some men might like to think about it. If even ten men thought it to feasible, it could help in reducing the age of acquiring a parish. I would not think that the bishop should be left with making such difficult decisions.

What is it that is attractive about becoming a parish priest? ... independence? power? control? These aspects of the position are enticing, admittedly, but somehow they cut across the notions of service, responsibility and team-ministry. Maybe we are still caught up in the boyhood dreams of being one's own person and not being controlled by a dean. All of this also points to the very simple fact that we, priests, are human and as such are subject to our human feelings and emotions.

There is a very special interlude in the 'autumnal years' for every priest ... the celebration of his Silver Jubilee. This special occasion is marked particularly by the people whom the priest is serving at the time. It is an occasion when most priests are bowled over by the love and generosity of their people. To have served for twenty-five years in the priesthood is as important as being married for twenty-five years. I remember when I once congratulated a priest on his silver jubilee, he simply said, 'Jimmy, I have survived, and sometimes it was like hanging on by my eyebrows!' Maybe this is one of the reasons that a priest desires to have a parish of his own ... he has been priesting for twenty-fve years and he is still an 'apprentice'. But it is a special stage in a priest's life and while there is a lot of joy surrounding it, there must also be deep inner feelings of loneliness ... no wife of one's own, no children of one's own, no home of one's own. And yet the Gospel passage which speaks of the follower of Jesus Christ as having given up wife, children, land, for the sake of Christ and the Gospel takes on a special significance now. The support of priest-friends and other close friends can be vitally important for a priest facing into his mid-life.

It is also a time in a priest's life when he may face a new crisis of faith brought upon him by the awareness of his life-state. If a priest's only solace has been the recitation of his breviary, he may begin to find the words of the psalms rather dry and boring. A friend of mine who is a layman once spoke to me of the fact that he found no experience of God when he went to Eucharist, that he looked up at the host at the consecration and simply wondered and questioned and his worry was that he was losing his faith. I spoke to him of his faith developing and growing and yet was aware that as I held that host in my hand each morning, I also wondered and questioned. I believe there is nothing more frightening for a priest that to experience grave, black doubts about his own faith and ministry. I am not talking here of the ordinary questioning that most people engage in, including priests. I am referring to the situation where a priest may find nothing but emptiness and blackness in his own life of prayer and sacramental administration. In this situation his whole life becomes a struggle and an effort. These are problems that many lay-people may experience ... they are problems of faith at its very basic. And it's not something which either a woman or power or security can erase ... they are problems of the inner heart of a person and they can be devastating. I personally knew of it for only a short period when I was learning to cope with my disease, but God then graced me in a special way ... at least that is my belief. A favourite line of one of the psalms used curdle in my head and heart, 'my only companion is darkness!' ... and it is not the most pleasant of companions. This darkness seemed to cover everything I did – saying Mass, hearing confessions, baptising, praying. It seemed to tear at the very roots of my living as it tore at the very roots of my priesthood.

Priests do not often talk of their struggles in faith, so I would not like to generalise or assume that this is the way for all priests. What I am saying is that the priest has to struggle with his faith as does the average lay-person. I could not put a time-limit on my own experience of darkness; I was not aware of time in days or weeks ... I was only aware of the intensity of the blackness and its searing pain. And while I found the experience to be difficult, thankfully I never gave up the fight for survival. I speak now of an awareness of God's presence with which I have been gifted ... it has to be a gift because it is none of my doing. Nor can I describe it very well apart from saying that I know there is a God, that he is a personal God, that his presence pervades everything and everybody, that there is no life without his presence. I have heard myself saying at times that God's presence bounces off the very pavements of the streets. So all that I can do now is to thank God for this gift and pray he never takes it from me ... and even with saying that I know that it is insufficient.

When a priest is struggling with his own faith and belief, it can be a very lonely struggle, because we are talking here of what goes on in the very depths of a man's heart and spirit and no-one can really enter that place except the person himself. And yet I know of priests who have been broken in spirit by life's experiences. They struggle with themselves and their God and may know of a deeper maturity out of it all. Doubts and questions about one's faith do not destroy it; they often help to deepen it provided one stays with the struggle. And yet it must seem a little strange for ordinary lay-people to imagine that one whose entire vocation and life is based on a faith in a personal God should have to struggle with that faith. I would be more unhappy about a man who is a priest and who never encounters difficulties with his own faith. If it is alive at all, then there has to be growth and development and these do not happen without some pain. As I have already said a priest may find his daily time-table taken up with so many things that he does not and is not able to give himself time for reflection and quiet.

This might be easier to understand if I tried to give a diary-like story of what often is a priest's day. For the sake of the story I will call the priest 'P' and simply give the other fictional characters initials by way of identification.

'P' arose after 8 o' clock to get himself ready for the 9 o' clock Mass. Just before he left the parochial house, a few letters came through his letter-box. He left them to be attended to after Mass. The usual dozen or so people were in their usual pews and 'P' was leaving the altar at 9.25 a.m. He said the Office of Readings and Morning Prayer from his breviary as his form of thanksgiving prayer, and was seated for his breakfast at 9.45 a.m. He opened his mail – an electricity bill, a telephone bill and a letter to inform him of the next priests' council meeting. He decided to leave his newspaper until lunch-time as he wanted to get to the primary school to meet the children preparing for confirmation. As he was about to leave the house at 10.15 a.m., the doorbell rang. The housekeeper announced that it was one of the workmen who was repairing the roof of the church. Apparently, the recent storm had done more damage than was first imagined which meant that a new estimate would have to be drawn up. Agreement was quickly reached on this.

'P' entered the primary school at 10.50 a.m. and was met by the principal who asked to see him for a few moments in the office. The Department of Education had informed him that as the school was dropping in numbers that there would be one redundant teacher in the new school year. As well as that the school would need to employ two new cleaning staff. The upshot of it all was that a meeting would have to be called to deal with these matters. The good news was that all had been arranged for the parents of the children for confirmation that night at 8.30 p.m. 'P' met the children at 11.15 a.m. and finalised the meeting for the parents with the teacher. Just as he was about to leave to visit the secondary school, the teacher asked him to call with her mother who had not been well. A note was made of it and 'P' reached the secondary school at 12 noon. There the principal told him of a little disquiet among the teachers about the recent allocation of posts. They chatted about it for a while until the head of the religious department asked to see him. One of the senior pupils had become pregnant and she would be willing to speak with 'P' about it. It was very typical of similar cases but no less difficult because of that. Her parents did not know; her boyfriend did not know and she felt that she could not cope. The visit took a little longer than he had thought and he did not arrive back for his lunch until 1.30 p.m.

He had a light lunch and then settled down to read the newspaper. The doorbell was ringing ... two Mass-cards to be signed, a baptismal form to be filled in and a call to visit Mr D. who had become ill. 'P' set out to meet with Mr D. and then to go on to call into the hospital. The sick-call was made and 'P' was in the hospital at 3.45 p.m. He had two particular people to see, one in ward 7 and the other in ward 2. As he stepped out of the elevator in ward 7, a young nurse asked to see him as she wanted to make an appointment to come to see him about getting her marriage papers prepared. The time was fixed and then he went to see Mrs S. who had been diagnosed as having cancer. She was in a ward with three other people and as was his wont, 'P' spent a little time with all of them. It was 4.45 p.m. by the time he got to ward 2. There his patient was in a ward with six other people. He was departing from the ward at 6.00 p.m. Just as he reached the car-park, a young man came running up to him pleading with him to visit his mother in ward 8. He would have liked to call at some other time but the young man was very persistent. 'P' agreed. It was 7.15 p.m. by the time he was sitting down for his evening meal. There were three telephone-calls – one from the bishop about the confirmation ceremony, one from a woman who said she was coming in at 8.00 p.m. to see him and one from Fr C about a golf match. He had just finished his tea when the doorbell rang and while the housekeeper was attending to it, he was able to telephone the bishop and Fr C. He looked at his watch as he approached the door of the call-room – 8.10 p.m. and he had to be at the school for the meeting with the parents at 8.30 p.m. The visitor wanting to see him was the mother of the young pregnant girl whom he had met earlier in the secondary school. He listened and advised as well as he could without allowing his own time-table to get in the way, but it was 9.00 p.m. by the time he reached the school. He knew that teacher M would be able to handle things until he came. There was a good turn-out of parents, but as usual there were four times as many women as men. 'P' tried to speak about the meaning of confirmation for parents and he tried to tackle it by trying to involve his audience in reflecting upon their own confirmations. He thought he spoke well and had posed a few questions for them to deal with and toss around. But their questions left 'P' wondering whether they has listened at all: 'Would there be tea and buns for the whole family after the confirmation Mass or would it be only for the confirmed children? Is it alright for a woman to be sponsor for a young boy? Must the children take the pledge to abstain from alcohol? Would the Mass last long? As the questions were being thrown about, he noticed Mrs. K sitting near the back. He knew that she was separated from her husband and was now living with a divorced man. 'It must have taken a lot of courage on her part to come here, tonight,' 'P' thought and decided to make a point of greeting her while the tea was being served. Then he remembered that he still had to call with the teacher's parent. This he did after the meeting and arrived back at the parochial house at 12 midnight. He finished his Office and got into bed at 1 a.m. He was awakened from his sleep at 3 a.m. and it was the young teacher to say that her mother had just died and would he mind calling to see the family as they were very upset. 'P' agreed and when the alarm went off at 8.00 a.m. next morning, it was a bit of a struggle to get out of bed. The usual dozen or so people were in their usual pews as he asked them to pray for the teacher's mother. And another day had begun.

Such days can be very real for the priest and as they accumulate, he can become very weary and tired. The golf match can help to get rid of some of the tension and the priest's own personal experience can help to cope with unknown stresses. Becoming a parish priest can often add to them rather than remove them. Every priest, no matter what his station is in the parish, will know of common stresses. I do want to say that I have great admiration for the priests in my own diocese, and that includes parish priests, but that does not mean that I would want to holiday with them all and I'm sure they feel the same towards me.

Priests can come in for a lot of criticism at times for the faults of the few. Yes, there are lazy priests, there are priests who do not care, there are priests who give people little time, there are priests who always seem to be away when people need them. But I believe it is more true and honest to say that the majority of priests give unselfish service twenty-four hours per day, seven days per week. Many priests work themselves into the ground for the sake of their people. And in spite of the criticism that is thrown at priests, I believe that people in general know of the great commitment shown by priests. Few people will hear of the priests who need medication or hospitalisation for burn-out and stress, because the priest will slip away, receive the necessary treatment, and return to his post again and only his closest priest-friends and family may be aware of it. I merely wish to put it on record here that priests can hold their heads high as they walk alongside their people and their people can rightly feel proud of them. This is in no way trying to justify the bad-tempered, crusty, ignorant, insensitive man who is wearing the collar. Such men may need to ask forgiveness of the people that they hurt and ask forgiveness of their fellow-priests whose good names they have damaged. But it is probably true to say that such men are not even aware of the trail of havoc which they leave in their wake. Nor do I wish to excuse them but I would like to redress the balance a little. There are people who can use the crusty priest as a reason for all the hurts and wrongs in our society.

I can still remember being thrown out of a confessional box. It was my second confession and I went in with 'my rhyme': 'Bless me Father, for I have sinned, it is my first confession ...' That was as far as I got. 'First confessions were last week, you silly little boy, now get out and prepare properly.' I went out as fast as I could and I did not stop running until I had reached my home. I still think the priest was wrong in what he did but that was the nature of the man and I was frightened of going to him for confession for many years after that. But I do not think it is a case for generalising about the wrongs of the Catholic Church. I'm sure everybody has a story about a priest that is far from pleasant and I would not like to see all mine being held up for ridicule. I am merely saying that if we call for the humanity of the priest to be seen, then we might not like what we see. To think or assume that the priest is a 'holy goodie - two - shoes' is making a big mistake.

I remember a story being told by a very fine priest and he was speaking about a preacher giving a mission in the parish. He stood up in the pulpit and was speaking of the awful reality of sin and of hell as being the possible consequence. He got carried away with his own rhetoric and began waving his arms about wildly. A little five year old boy moved slowly closer to his mother. The priest's face got redder, his voice began to shriek somewhat, his arms made mighty sweeps in the air. The little boy tugged at his mother's arm and asked in a loud whisper, 'What will happen, Mammy, if he escapes?' It is a good story and yet one may ask 'What will happen to that little boy because of that experience?' I trust his parents will be wise and have good sense and that he meets the ordinary, good, conscientious and caring priest... and there are many of them around.

I would like to say here also that it is to the credit of the middle-aged priest that he still has enough enthusiasm to desire the responsibilities and obligations of a parish. I would not like to give the impression that I am knocking a priest for wanting and looking forward to becoming a parish priest. I know that if I were not ill that I would be looking forward to the challenge of such a position. Priests generally take on this challenge with a good heart and a strong desire to serve their new people. He has to begin all over again, maybe for the fourth or fifth time in his life, to get to know an entirely new group of people and it does not get any easier as the years go on. Hopefully he learns to cope with and adapt to the 'season of mist and mellow fruitfulness' and grows to the fulness of his own humanity without compromising either himself or the message he has been sent to preach. Autumn in nature continually surprises us with its warm, strong colours, its strange and beautiful sunsets, its sudden storms and calming breezes. The human person when he/she reaches the 'autumnal years' is often a good person to be with. They are able to relax, enjoy a good brandy or cigar and can talk from a lot of experience. Their stories are plentiful and interesting and contain new turns of phrase that would delight Joyce himself. So too for the priest who has matured through the storms of his life and is still prepared to listen and learn. And as the month of September approaches (the month when changes are announced in our diocese) the priest begins to wonder about his 'new parish'. He may become a bit untidy with his own parish as he tries not to take on any new work which he may not be able to finish. It could be the one change he looks forward to with a new inner spark and glow. He may not look forward to the goodbyes but he is anxious about the new challenges that will face him.

The Winter

I wonder why we often think of the winter as 'a season of discontent'. It is another stage in a person's growth and development. There can be the cruel mornings of frost and black ice patches on the road. But similarly there can be the gentle fall of the first snow bestowing a white mantle on the green fields and tall mountains. There can be the fresh, delicate breeze that cuts into the skin and makes one don the heavy coat and warm scarf. The new parish has been accepted and the priest begins once again to pack his books and belongings, hoping that this will be the last time for such things. No change is ever easy for the priest as he prepares to say goodbye once again.

People sometimes ask why a priest should ever be changed from a parish. I think there may be several good reasons that change take place. The priest himself may need the change because if he has been in the parish for a long time, he can easily fall into a rut. He develops a routine way of doing things and he may find it hard to change his habits. A change of a parish can give him some new life and energy. The people may need the change as they have become too accustomed to the priest and no matter how brilliant he may be, he soon runs out of new things to say. It is also true that a priest may find himself circulating with the same people on too regular a basis and other people may find this difficult to accept. It could be that the priest has hurt a number of people, even unintentionally, and they find it particularly difficult to relate not only to the priest but to what they would call 'the Church'. These are some of the ordinary and human reasons why it can be a good thing for the priest to be changed from a parish in which he has served for a number of years. It may not make the change any easier for the priest or the people. There is always some process of dying that takes place as the priest uproots himself from a people whom he has loved and served. It carries its own form of pain with which a priest has to learn to deal. There is an unhealthy side to it as well, as a priest may be loathe to form or develop new relationships in each parish because he knows that he will eventually be moved. Once the priest has arrived at his new parish as the pastor, he may feel that he can now lay down more permanent roots.

So the new parish priest begins to establish himself. He usually finds that there can be plenty of jobs to be done as the previous parish priest may have done little in the parish for some years ... the church may need renovations, repairs may be needed for the parochial house or the parochial hall, liturgical reforms may be needed, new committees may need to be established. All of these operations and others like them give the new priest plenty of opportunities for meeting the people and getting to know them. He may face certain opposition from well established groupings as they fear that their 'power' is being taken away from them. When I was establishing myself as Administrator of St Mary's, Creggan, and began introducing new people into various groupings, the comment was made that 'new kings make new laws'. I had to be aware of hurting people and yet try to move forward with some of my ideas. I can remember sitting with my three curates as we reorganised the Sunday Masses while the church was being renovated and actually feeling a little fright as the times of Masses would be affecting hundreds of people. It seemed like a lot of power to have for such a young man. We tried to keep the people's needs in mind as we came to our decisions. It was making such decisions as these that I found the parish council to be of such benefit. What I did find strange was the fact that I was responsible for large sums of money – and spending it wisely was as difficult as raising it. I never thought that I would be running bingo games. I had only ever been at one bingo game when I was a young student – as chaperon to my mother. She was disgusted because I took a novel along with me to read during the games. I was grateful for the novel; otherwise I would have been totally bored out of my mind. But then I found that I was responsible for running such games. I made a deal with the organising committee. They would be in charge of the running of the games; they made the decisions about prizes, they distributed the prize-money and they met with me each week (at least one of them to keep me informed of matters) and I would visit the hall at least twice per year to render thanks formally to the participants ... and a few unofficial calls were always welcomed by both the committee and the people.

Beginning in a new parish is a very important time and I think that a lot of thought should be given to the parish priest's first sermon. First impressions are always important and the same applies to this situation. I had been working as diocesan secretary when the bishop told me that he was appointing me as Administrator to Creggan. I was given about six or seven weeks' notice of the change and I gave a lot of thought to the first words which I would share with my new people. And even though I was a priest of eleven years I was still a bit frightened as I walked out onto the sanctuary and looked down at a congregation of about a thousand people. At the homily time, I told them that all that I had to offer them was myself, but that I would be asking them to share their gifts with me. I asked the old people for the gift of faith. They had persevered in the faith for many, many years and they are often the people who spend a lot of their time at prayer. They are the people who still think it important to pay a visit to the church; they clutch their rosaries more tightly than their purses or wallets. I remember a revered old parish priest once tell me of his visit one day to an old man in his parish. It was the afternoon when he called in to see him. The old man was sitting quietly by his fireside with his rosary beads in his hand. 'Sit down, father',.said he, 'I'm talking to the boss and I'll be with you in a moment.' Somehow the parish priest knew that it would be an intrusion to ask to join the man in his prayer, so he waited patiently for him to finish. There is something special about an old person's prayer – they often seem to be in close touch with God himself. I would believe that to be one of their predominant features. They have other less pleasant ones as they too are only human. I remember being asked by a married lady to visit her sick mother who would probably need to be put on my 'sick-list' so that I could bring communion to her each month. So I began going to the old lady's home to meet with her and make the appropriate arrangements. I called at the house at morning time, in the afternoon and at night for several weeks but

could never find her. I met her accidently at one of the parish
dances. 'Hello, father, I believe you were down at the house looking for me,' she said. 'Yes,' I said, 'I was beginning to get worried
about you. I even rang the hospital in case you had been admitted.' 'Not at all, father,' she said, 'you see, in the mornings I go out
to do my shopping; in the afternoons I visit one of my daughters,
and most nights of the week I go to play bingo.' 'But I thought you
were ill or something,' I said, feeling a bit foolish. 'Well, you see,
it's like this. I get very claustrophobic in the chapel and I would
like you to visit me in my home,' said she. I had learned in my
priesthood about what I would call 'chapel claustrophobia' – a
fear of being confined in a place where there may be a lot of people
and a lot of silence!

But back to my homily. I asked the married people for the gift of
love. They are in the business of living it at close range and expressing it by their life-long commitment. I needed the witness of
their fidelity.

I asked the youth for the gift of hope. They are the people who can
dream and wish for better things from life and they are cour-
ageous enough to risk. I needed them to challenge me and help me
to broaden my horizons.

And finally I asked the children for the gift of joy and laughter.
They still have the innocence of being able to smile on a dreary
day.

As I finished I was completely amazed at the reception which I received ... the congregation stood up and applauded. I was dumb-
founded and felt tears come to my eyes as I tried to lead them in the
recitation of the Creed. I am sorry now that I fought back those
tears so successfully. I think they may have been very appropriate. But a good connection was made immediately. The memory
of that event helped me when times got rough and certainly encouraged me to tell those people before I left them that I loved
them. I know that is a thing that priests do not do normally and yet
if it is true I wonder why it is not expressed. When a priest has been
in a parish for a certain length of time I believe that a love relation-

ship grows between himself and his people. It is something which encourages a priest to continue serving. How is it possible for a priest to celebrate the eucharist consistently with a group of people, share the very food of life with them regularly and not come to love them? It is because of this love that he finds it within himself to 'scold' his people and to call them back to the way of life that is appropriate for a believing people. The priest who 'scolds' out of anger has got something wrong.

A priest's 'anger' is a strange sort of commodity. He has as much right to his anger as anybody else but he has no right to put out his own private anger onto his people. If he allows his anger to permeate his Sunday homily he is truly abusing his 'pulpit right'. It can happen that a priest is disturbed out of his Saturday night sleep by a drunken person at the door, but to use that as an excuse to 'give off' to his people about parish drinking is in itself immoderate. The drunk can be a very difficult person to deal with at any time and he/she can become a totally irrational person who would tax the patience of Job himself. I have had explosions of temper from time to time between myself and an individual but I have been able to go to those people afterwards and effect a reconciliation. Those matters were private and I hope I did not take it out on my people ... and thankfully I can say that not many people have seen that anger or indeed felt it. We all have heard stories about priests losing their tempers within the confessional area. This I find hard to understand and I would not try to defend it. I am still amazed when I hear of priests who become angry because of the nature of sins that are confessed. This anger is indefensible. The only time that I can remember being pushed to the edge in the confessional was one particular Christmas. We had been hearing confessions and we began on Christmas Eve at 11.00 a.m. and we were leaving our boxes at 2.30 p.m. After lunch, hospital visitation still had to be done and confessions resumed at 6.00 p.m. There were queues waiting at our boxes when we entered the Church at six o' clock. There was not one break as we 'shuttled' the people in and out. At about 10.30 p.m., I was able to sense from the prevailing silence in the church that we were coming near the end. Finally the last person entered the box. I was tired and weary but took a

deep breath thinking that this might be a person who has struggled with him/herself about coming at all. I pushed back the grill
and waited. 'Excuse me, father,' said a lady, 'I don't wish to go to
confession but I wonder would you sign a Mass bouquet for me
which I wish to give as a wee Christmas present ?' As I switched
on the light and grunted a 'yes', an envelope was pushed under
the grill towards me … I opened it and found fifteen Mass bouquet
cards for signing. I signed them alright but I'm sure that nobody
could have read my signature. I felt like exploding, but I didn't... I
waited until I got back to the parochial house before emitting a
scream. And that was only my second Christmas as a priest. Mass
cards and the like still bug me a little in the confessional but I have
nothing but admiration for the person who comes to confession
and with honesty and courage entrusts him/herself to a priest for
the forgiveness of God.

Meanwhile the new parish priest settles himself into the parish
and slowly but surely stamps his mark on the place. Sometimes I
am still amazed at how much influence a parish priest can have on
people. I do not know if this is peculiar to Ireland but in my experience it seems to be that no matter how hardworking, caring,
responsible the curate(s) may be, it is still the parish priest whose
influence is felt and whose words will be quoted. If the parish
priest does not agree with something then that becomes the last
word on the subject. I suppose it could be said that this places
more responsibility on the parish priest to be aware of what he
does and says.

However after a number of years, the renovations are completed,
the excitement has cooled as the ordinary parish routine matters
take up more of his time and the parish priest may begin to become more aware of his own aging. He is no longer able to take the
stairs two at a time, he must spread out his monthly sick calls over
a number of days as his energy is lower, the afternoon nap becomes a necessity rather than a luxury. He begins to notice other
things in himself which make him begin to wonder … crying babies
in chapel are now a nuisance, young brides consistently coming
late for their weddings annoy him, first confessions become try-

ing and people standing in the porch of the church are an insult to Jesus! Younger priests can also identify with some of these 'nuis- ances' but there is less spark in the older priest to be able to deal with them. However his experience and common sense are often bigger than the younger priest's and he can survive in spite of them.

After a while he may begin to realise that many of his age-group are either retiring or dying and he must begin to face into his own winter. If he has stuck at his post for over fifty years he knows that he will soon be getting a letter from his bishop informing him that he is due to retire. This cannot be easy for him as he wonders what he will do with himself. I heard of a parish priest referring to his re- tirement as 'his dying'. I can understand to some extent what must be going on in his mind and heart. Due to my own illness, I had to relinquish all normal parish work and it was not easy letting it all go at forty-two years of age. I am still a priest and find that my days and hours are still pretty full but it is a completely different kind of work, and maybe because I am still 'fairly young' I am more able to adapt to the changing conditions. While the diocese still ensures that the retiring priest is looked after from a material point of view, I'm not so sure that all their needs are being met. If even one of those men should feel that he is 'being dumped', then something is wrong. They are given the opportunity of becoming curates again if they should so wish but it could not be easy for a man of seventy-five to go to another parish and begin again, and to stay on in his own parish with a new parish priest coming in could lead to difficulties for both men. But I am really talking about the special caring of and tending to the older men that might need to be looked at. It just cannot be easy to stop doing the things one had been doing for fifty years and be given the title 'pastor emeritus'. Older priests do not talk much about this subject and it might be useful if they did and so prepare the way for much more indepth thought on the subject of retirement. Modern sciences are spending a lot of time and energy on the whole subject of death it- self which is encouraging to all of us who must face that moment ourselves. And maybe the point I made earlier about 'retiring' to be a curate at sixty-five has some meaning at this stage. 'Once a

priest, always a priest' is still part of our theology and that is perfectly true, but how much of a priest's life is tied up with a parish
and all that means, and to suddenly find that all of that is finished
must have serious repercussions to the inner self-worth and es-
teem of the older retiring man. What does he do with his time?
And if a priest has not picked up a few hobbies along the way, he
could find life a bit boring if all that he has to look forward to is the
daily paper and television.

I have sometimes wondered about the wealth of experience that
the older priests have and how that could be put to better us. They
must have a lot to offer the springtime men and yet there may be
simply an age barrier here that would prevent real communication. I remember visiting an old retired priest and after we had exchanged all the niceties, I asked him had he many visitors.
'Enough,' he said, 'but I would prefer if I did not see any of the wee
young fellows and I simply have to say to the bishop that I am
tired, for him to leave.' He wanted to be alone and was content
with himself to be alone. And men have a right to their privacy if
that is their wish and I am certainly not trying to construct some
new system to 'help them adjust to their retirement'. In fact all that
I am trying to say is that it could be very important that we know
the needs of the retiring men and then respond to those needs. A
priest may want more than a roof over his head and a monthly
cheque coming in his letterbox.

However this is not meant to be a 'white paper' and I hope it is not
read as such. I remember when my own father retired that he was
glad of the few voluntary activities in which he was involved and
he persevered with those until his own health broke. Getting
ready for his 'meeting nights' became a type of ritual for him and
it was important to him that his advice and wisdom were being
sought. Of course, he had his grand-children who gave him a lot
of joy and it was a beautiful experience for me to witness him playing with them... and thinking that that must have been how he
played with me when I was a child. It reminds me of the story of
the old priest who was speaking to a group of clerical students.
When they asked him did he think that celibacy would be

changed, he replied, 'Well, young men, I think it will change some time but not in either your life-time or mine … but our children may live to see the day.' I wonder do priests think about who will remember them, apart from their own families, and what happens to the man whose parents are dead and who has no brothers or sisters? I sometimes think of the old priests, who had such power and influence in the diocese when I was a young priest, and after only one year of their deaths, they seemed to be easily forgotten. But as one critical observer said to me, 'c'est la vie, c'est la mors!'

The Future

If I have sketched an unusual 'year' in the life-time of a priest, I wonder, like many others, what will the future hold. Here in Ireland we have a fairly fixed way of being a priest. When a priest is changed from one parish to another, it takes some time to be able to let go of his former parish and a little more time to get his bearings in the new parish. The people will have changed but the life-style of the priest will remain fairly static. He gets to know his sick-run, the schools of the parish, the usual parish organisations, and just takes up from where his predecessor left off. The only new challenges will be the new faces that he has to deal with. The usual problems and responsibilities will come up, but he has faced them all before and it will not be long before he has fixed for himself a working schedule.

Yet I wonder is this how it should be or even can be. The N.C.P.I. renewal courses for Irish priests are attracting more and more men today. I attended this course back in 1984 and was enthused not only by the course itself but by the men who were attending it. There was a broad spectrum of ages on the course and every man seemed to want some direction on his future. There was due emphasis on the eight-day directed retreat in the middle of the course. This emphasis on the inner heart of the man who is the priest was like the main artery running through the entire course. Renewal begins within the person and the priest is no exception. But if new wine is poured into old wine-skins, might there not be the possibility of both being lost?

Is today's Irish Church being challenged to look at its own structures and to change whatever needs to be changed? Everyone is a little frightened of change because it can reveal a person's deep insecurities. The Second Vatican Council made a lot of changes and most people experienced these in the revised liturgical changes. Some people and priests are still trying to come to terms with eucharistic ministers, lay-readers, even communion in the hand. And yet many of these changes are purely functional.

While the renewal of the priest is being directed at his inner self, is it possible that the priest in Ireland might have to change the practice of his role as leader? Can we simply hope that our priests will deepen their own spirituality and revise their relationship with Christ and not look at how they operate within the parish structure?

The parish as we know it has served the Church well for many years. Its structures and systems have allowed priest and people to work together in some form of acceptable relationship and it would be foolish to throw out what has been a good way of being together. But we are hearing new words which may make new demands on the priest of the next millenium. A word used by Popes in recent years has been the word, 'evangelisation'. Can we afford to pretend that it is not important? And if it is, what will it demand of the priest in the parish?

Some may think that this has only to do with the new and up and coming generations and therefore merely a matter of catechetics in the school. How widespread is the break-down in faith practice among our young people? Many of them openly admit to slack Sunday worship. Their attendance of Sunday eucharist would be intermittent and occasional. Yet they show willingness to attend voluntary faith growth classes and express a desire to know more about the faith. One young person said to me recently that she is pleased with having the possibility of such 'classes' and went on to say that her mother is somewhat envious of such an opportunity.

Would other adults welcome the opportunity of being able to come together to discuss scripture, liturgy, and morality? Societies like St Vincent de Paul and The Legion of Mary are well-founded and serve a good purpose, but might there not be room for something more?

The values of the normal parish system are important but it leads to the priest being a sort of 'maintenance' man. He attends to things as they happen and makes sure that the people are serviced with Mass, confessions and other liturgical celebrations. He may

be challenged to think and use his intelligence each weekend as
he struggles with the Sunday scripture to prepare his homily. If he
does not even do this, then he may find that he is simply repeating
some of his well-worn ideas from past homilies and neither he nor
his congregation are fed by the word of God.

One of the points put to the priests on the N.C.P.I. course in 1984
was that the priest see himself as a 'talent-scout'. The priest of the
future may need to discern in more acute fashion the needs of the
parish and then to try to respond to meet them. Almost twenty
years ago, another priest and myself were asked to examine the
then current situation about marriage in the diocese. The end result of a lot of hard work was to up-date marriage preparation
courses, and have people trained in the skills of counselling in
marital relationship. The Catholic Marriage Advisory Council
was eventually formed in the diocese. This was a recognition that
the priest may not always be the best person to help in a difficult
marriage problem; and also we recognised the fact that good,
competent lay-people may need some particular training. In a
sense this was a form of talent scouting, seeking out those people
who might be suitable in this particular field and then equipping
them with the necessary tools and skills for such work.

But just as priests today are anxious about their own personal renewal, I would suggest that our people are similarly hungry. Our
people are no longer content with a dry empty practice of their
faith; they too are seeking a warm and personal relationship with
their God. They have shown themselves willing to accept the many
liturgical changes that have happened since Vatican II, but they
are thirsting for the new thinking and 'aggiornamento' that is behind the external changes. I am reminded of the Gospel story
which recounts the meeting between Jesus and the woman at the
well, in John 4ff. In that Gospel Jesus says, 'The hour will come
when true worshippers will worship in spirit and truth.' I get the
strong sense that our people are thirsting for the true heart of reli-
gion and I doubt if we are supplying the right water which would
give sustenance to that growth. In order to effect this renewal
within the parish set-up, the priest may need to 'scout' around his

parish and find helpers who would be willing to do what is necessary in order to create a spirit of renewal. Such people could eventually become the leaven within the parish to work with the priest in setting up a programme of evangelisation for the parish. Many of our people are waiting for the right lead and they are looking to their priests for that lead. Such inner renewal among priests and people would revitalise parish life both liturgically and socially. It would not be a question of the priest having all the answers, but more a question of priest and people searching together. I know this will involve new structures and a new way of communicating between priests and people, but I do not believe we have any other option. We have ploughed the same ground over and over again; now we must plant anew. I still see the value of societies like St Vincent de Paul and, to a lesser extent, the Legion of Mary. But as someone said recently, it is not devotions to Mary we should be supporting but devotion to Mary. She was a young lady filled with God's Spirit, a woman who was able to make great space for God, first of all in her heart. God's Spirit challenges every person. When challenged I must stop and declare myself, as did Mary. The answer to the challenge will always be the same ultimately; the approach to the answer will be different. Are we willing to change our approaches today? While the old pattern of parishes have served us well, I question whether we can afford to stay within the old pyramid-like paradigm in which all decisions are taken at the top and then passed down to those 'below'.

There seems to be a crying need for a new way of relating between priests and people which acknowledges each one's position and dignity. There is some talk today about team-ministry which allows the priest to attend to his work and his own special field and encourages the laity to take their rightful responsibility within the modern parish structure. The old system of priest 'being in charge' is no longer truly adequate. Life questions the Gospel and the Gospel questions life. In our day the Spirit is not a passive source of peace but it is an actual living involvement of a living God involved in life. We are not priests alone, we hold priesthood with Jesus Christ and with the brotherhood of priests and with the priesthood of the laity and, lest we forget, the women are as much part of the priesthood of the laity as the men. We may feel we have involved them in parish structures by allowing them to become lay-ministers of the Eucharist and lay-readers, but if our attitude is that we have merely promoted them to 'more important' duties, perhaps we still see them as good tea-ladies. It would be extremely interesting to listen to women about how they view themselves within parish and it might be frightening for us to listen.

We are called to become vehicles of God's power. And we share in the mission of Jesus Christ; sent to do the will of the Father in establishing and spreading the kingdom of God, a kingdom of justice, love and peace. Christ was as human as we are; he knew all human experience; he loved life and, day by day, Christ was moulded by the Spirit in the midst of life. We are ordained priests but we are being shaped more and more into a priestly person by the Spirit of God in life.

A task for the priest today is to learn to live reflectively, to pause, to think, and to speak of the deep things of God. Sadly a priest can often be identified with the law of God and not the person of God. Priests may need to learn to walk by a different wisdom. Jesus learned from his desert experience to be led by the Spirit; he had to learn the emptiness of worldly power, the poverty of being a man, the need to rely totally on the wisdom and power of God. Priests can learn to know that, from their own lives of exasperation, sadness, frustration, joy and sometimes seemingly futile effort. We are called to stay with that experience and in the midst of struggle to remember that Christ redeemed the world by what is often called failure, death on a cross. This philosophy, theology, call it what you want, is the source of the priest's effectiveness, power and strength. But to live this will need the support of others, the support of fellow-priests, the support of willing lay-people. I believe it is available.

Obviously this will make new demands of the priest; it will challenge his spirituality in a way that will be different. Every year the priest goes off for four or five days for his own retreat. I personally have quite enjoyed the retreats which I have experienced these past number of years; but the emphasis is a little unbalanced.

These few special days can sometimes be a way of getting in touch with new theological developments within the Church or simply seen as a time when a priest looks after his own soul, makes a good confession and a few resolutions about his life, renews old friendships and returns with a lighter heart to his parish. There are few opportunities for a priest to try to deepen his own spirituality on an on-going basis. Some priests are already trying to fill this lacuna by voluntarily joining priests' fraternities, priests' prayer groups and homiletic groups. This is all to the good, and yet I feel there could be more encouragement and direction given to such groupings without trying to control them.

A few years ago, I was visiting Dublin to meet with a couple of postulants. They invited me to go to Mass with them at St Kevin's Church but warned me that we would need to go almost an hour before the Mass would begin. I did as they suggested and was quite taken by the spirit of prayer and celebration of that eucharist. The fact that the majority of the faithful who were present that particular evening were young people was something special to witness. There was nothing different about the way Mass was celebrated, but the setting, the music, the overall community feeling was strong and vibrant. I'm sure a lot of work had gone in to such a gathering, but it was well worth it.

This is a challenging and hopeful time. I have no clear ideal of how this vision can be put into practice on the ground, but I believe this is the calling of today's Church. We have seen the kerygmatic renewal sparked off by the charismatic movement; we have witnessed the new ways of the encounter movements; we are experiencing the growth of the Cursillo movement; and alongside all of these has been the mushrooming of priest and lay 'Jesus Caritas' fraternity groupings. These have been and are signs of the times and the groanings of the Spirit moving in the Church today.

People could sit back and mourn about the fragile nature of today's church structures; on the other hand it is just as easy to see tiny signs of life and vitality; little buds seeking water for growth and needing tender care and nurturing. Can we afford to continue simply as maintenance men?

I think of the early Church in apostolic times; how it grew out of small communities, communities that were given leadership and strong guidance by men and women alive with the Spirit of God. Is it impractical to think of small street or estate groups meeting together to prayerfully search for renewal, evangelisation, Gospel sharing? And if that were to happen, such groupings would need the help of good leaders who would encourage, support and strengthen Christian living and loving. Is it impossible to think that priests could 'talent scout' and select such leaders from within their parishes and, after effective preparation, work with these same people on a prepared programme? Many dioceses are buzzing with Adult Religious Education classes. But what happens to such dedicated lay-people after two years' study? Are we being fair to them by giving them intensive and extensive study classes without any thought being given to a local missionary apostolate? I have met many such people who, after having undergone a course in Adult Religious Education, ask the very pertinent question, 'How can we be of help now in the parish, father?' In a very real sense we have already been moved along the road of personal renewal (moved, need I say by the Spirit of God) and I believe we are being invited to follow that road. The Church, the People of God, is very much alive. We know what happened to Jesus Christ when he was 'driven' by the Spirit and we know that the journey might not be a pleasant one, but can we afford to refuse the invitation?

I think back to my experience in Waterside parish in the early seventies. The parish was in the process of setting up a Parish Council. The priests felt at that time that we needed help from the laity. We gathered together a working-team of men and women from the parish to consider the nature of a Parish Council. This team worked closely with the priests for some months, examining Vatican Council documents and other literature available at that time. The team of laity also volunteered to go around the parish and meet with the people from the various areas in order to explain what they themselves had learned. One of the priests was usually present at these meetings. The interesting thing was that it was the lay-person who gave the talk at the meeting and then chaired the discussion. Finally the team agreed to look after the elections to the Council and then voluntarily disbanded as a committee. It created tremendous enthusiasm within the parish itself and led to a great spirit of togetherness. While all this was going on, parish work continued as usual – the sick, hospitals, schools and homes were visited.

When I was appointed to Creggan parish in 1978, one of the projects undertaken by the parish council there was the selection and training of lay eucharistic ministers. The parish council was comprised of the four priests, several laymen and lay women. It was decided to talk to the general body of parishioners at Sunday Mass over a period of a few weeks. When the lay ministers had been selected, they were asked to attend a diocesan day of preparation; but they also asked their priests to give them some more preparation. Each of us, the four priests, met with them, gave a talk on some aspect of the eucharist, and finally all of us came together to discuss practical tips and to decide on a rota of Mass-time for each lay minister. The lay people elected a coordinator from among their own ranks, a person who would handle little practical difficulties about times and absenteeism. They did this, as they said, so that we, their priests, would not have to worry or be troubled with such incidental matters. It reminded me a little of the selection of the deacons in the Acts of the Apostles, so that the apostles could concentrate on their role of preaching and teaching. We decided as a group to come together about twice a year for prayer, reflection and to discuss any practical difficulties that may have arisen. We did the same with our lay readers and one of the priests took responsibility for the on-going training of such people.

I think of the amount of time which many a priest has to spend at administrative meetings. If a priest is 'in charge of' a busy parish, he will discover that he has to spend many days and nights chairing meetings. It is said that a priest has to be chairman of the school committee to ensure that a Catholic ethos is maintained within the school. But surely committed Catholic parents and teachers are as concerned, if not more concerned, that the pupils of a Catholic school receive a good Catholic education as much as the priest? In other parts of the Catholic world where priests are not as numerous as in Ireland, other committed lay-people take over such responsibilities, so that the priest can take his proper role as animator, spiritual guide, and 'father' of his people. A parish office with a few committed personnel could adequately manage many of the administrative duties now looked after by the priest.

When we worked with our groups of laity in Creggan parish and involved them in parish ministries, almost imperceptibly a strong parish bond grew between these groups and the priests that filtered down through the whole parish. A word that I would use to describe it is 'belonging' – all of us felt we belonged to each other and to a living Church. I would be able to look back and see how this attitude affected our sacramental liturgy. Baptism was the sacrament that brought us together into the one family; eucharist was the sacrament that continually re-enforced that sense of belonging – we ate at the same table and were fed with the unifying Body of Christ. We became the Body of Christ, each with his/her own particular ministry. It was as if we were putting into practice the Pauline theology of the Mystical Body of Christ, in very simple but effective ways.

I am reminded of the prayer in Psalm 51: 'God, create a clean heart in me, put into me a new and constant spirit,' and of a few lines earlier in the same psalm: 'Since you love sincerity of heart, teach me the secrets of wisdom.' We are being constantly asked to trust God – We so the planting, he does the growing. In Jeremiah, 31, v.33, we read: 'Deep within them I will plant my Law, writing it on their hearts. Then I will be their God and they shall be my people.' Such a text speaks of the vision which I have for the Church – impossible for the human person, but not for God. We are being asked to push out a little into the deep and to trust, not in our own foibles and imperfections, which are worthless anyway, but to trust in the very power of God himself. He has not abandoned us; he cannot.

To work with small groups willing to search in prayer with the priest is surely the way forward. And with such a spirit pervading parish life, I do not think that the maintenance work will suffer. Anyway it would be more catastrophic to risk God's Spirit being stifled by working out of the wrong vision. Maybe that is what is needed at this moment – for someone to work at and write out the vision-mission of a parish.

Evangelisation is not merely about teaching people commandments, precepts, ordinances; it is that but much more. It is about creating new hearts and new spirits, out of which will blossom new ways of acting and behaving. 'By their fruits you shall know them,' was how Jesus declared recognition of his followers. 'I am the vine, you are the branches,' is a familiar Gospel phrase about the relationship between us and the Father. The Life-Spirit of God moves through our very selves to enliven and empower us. Evangelisation is about helping us to be rooted in the God-life by a new way of relating with the Father, through Jesus Christ in the Spirit. I do not see it as destroying the parish structure, but as re-creating it and using it to its full potential. In fact I would say that we are blessed with having such a strong fabric on which to work – but at times men and women have felt that when dealing with parish life and parishioners, it is a bit like dealing with dry bones which need refleshed and given life.

It is unthinkable that such could happen? What work might be involved in such pastoral planning and re-modelling? We already have good strong parish structures and fairly good relationships between our priests and people, but do we use them as we could? I'm thinking about what are usually called parish missions – we ask our people every few years to come to church and to be preached at for an extended period with the hope that some lapsed Catholics might return to the sacraments. Might such exercises be revamped so as to enable priests and people to be rejuvenated and filled again with new purpose and new hope? I have seen churches filled to over-flowing when speakers such as Sister Breige McKenna and Father Kevin Scallon speak to them of God's love and power.

Our people are thirsting for new life and new commitment and they are ready to respond. Are we ready to give and to supply what ourselves and our people need? *Nemo dat quod non habet*, is a Latin phrase with which every priest would be familiar – 'No-one gives what he does not have.' If our people are to be renewed, it is important that we, their priests, have the same experience. Wouldn't it be challenging if we undertook such renewal together?

Today it is easy to see people who have just completed some spiritual exercise. They come away enthused and even excited, and there is need for that same spirit of enthusiasm to sweep through our parish communities. Priests and people together can recapture that sense of excitement about the presence of the Risen Lord in their midst. We, who have ever been deeply touched by some spiritual experience, rarely reflect upon the fact that we have been touched by God himself; we shy away from the idea that we have experienced the hand of God.

This is an exciting time for the Church; slowly some priests are preparing themselves; slowly groups of the laity are exercising their right to deepen their relationship with God. Why cannot we do this together? The Church is a pilgrim Church on the move; all of us make up The People of God and we are on the same road, travelling together, stumbling together but with the same objective in view – to establish God's kingdom in our hearts and in our parishes, and then hopefully to enjoy the fulness of God's kingdom in our eternal home. Why not help one another, support one another and learn to lean more on each other? For the priest, it will probably mean forfeiting his role as authority figure and controller and trying to learn to be a spiritual focus and guide for his people. For our laity, it may mean loving in a deeper way their Fathers in Christ. 'Maranatha' (Come, Lord Jesus!) was a prayer of the early Christian communities; it could be a useful cry and prayer of the modern-day Christian. Exciting? Yes; Challenging? Yes; Daunting? Yes; but if the Lord is on our side, what or who have we to fear?